In The Palm of His Hand

In The Palm of His Hand

The History of St. Joseph's Catholic Church
Pine Bluff, Arkansas
1838–1984

Eleanor Rucks Lambert

May He put you in His angel's charge
To guard you all your days.
May He raise you up on eagle's wings,
And hold you in the palm of His hand.

Based on Psalm 91

Copyright 1985 by St. Joseph's Catholic Church, Pine Bluff,
Arkansas. Published 1985 by August House, Inc., Publishers,
Post Office Box 3223, Little Rock, Arkansas 72203. 501-663-
7300. All rights reserved; no part of this book may be
reproduced in any manner without the prior written consent of
St. Joseph's Catholic Church. Manufactured in the United States
of America.

First Edition 1985.

TO ORDER ADDITIONAL COPIES:

Send $14.98 + $1.25 Postage and Handling in check or money order to:

ST. JOSEPH'S CATHOLIC CHURCH
P.O. Box 7434
Pine Bluff, Arkansas 71601

Library of Congress Cataloging-in-Publication Data
Lambert, Eleanor Rucks, 1924–
   In the palm of His hand.

   Bibliography: p.
   Includes index.
   1. St. Joseph's Catholic Church (Pine Bluff, Ark.)—
History. 2. Pine Bluff (Ark.)—Church history.
I. Title.
BX4603.P535S75   1985   282'.76779   85-9036
ISBN 0-935304-92-4

Contents

Message from His Excellency, Bishop Andrew J. McDonald, D.D	7
Message from the Very Reverend Leo A. Riedmueller, V.F.	9
Preface	11
1. Catholic Missionaries in Arkansas	13
2. St. Mary's Settlement	16
3. St. Mary's, Plum Bayou and Cemetery Records	22
4. St. Peter's, New Gascony and Cemetery Records	28
5. Old French Cemetery	31
6. Early Catholic Families	33
7. St. Joseph's Church, Pullen and Georgia Streets	40
8. St. Joseph's Church, West Sixth Avenue	44
9. St. Joseph's Church, 1923 to the Present Time	57
10. Associate Pastors, 1908–1984	65
11. Memorials	67
12. The Priests of St. Joseph's	71
13. The Sisters of St. Joseph's	84
14. The Deacons of St. Joseph's	91
15. The Priests from St. Joseph's Parish	95
16. The Sisters from St. Joseph's Parish	103
17. The Bishops of the Diocese of Little Rock	105
18. Annunciation Academy, St. Joseph's School, Pine Bluff Catholic School and Convent Chapel	116
19. St. Joseph's Cemetery and Interments 1840–1913	120
20. Laymen of St. Joseph's Church	136
21. St. Peter's Mission	138
22. Blessed Sacrament Church, Grady, Arkansas and Cemetery Records, St. Paul's Church, Noble Lake, St. Patrick's Church, Sulphur Springs	140
23. Parish Religious Education	144
24. Church Organizations	146
25. The 1984 Parish Council	154
26. The Staff of St. Joseph's	156
27. Organists of St. Joseph's	158
Footnotes	159
Index	170

The Most Reverend Andrew J. McDonald, D.D., Bishop of Little Rock.

DIOCESE OF LITTLE ROCK
2415 North Tyler Street
P. O. Box 7239, Forest Park Station
LITTLE ROCK, ARKANSAS 72217

Telephone
Area Code 501
664-0340

Office of the Bishop

January 27, 1984

Dear Friends in Christ:

    If we search the holy Bible, we will find the Lord present in the desert, on the mountains, near the rivers. The Lord was present among His people when the Catholic Church began its work in the State of Arkansas.

    In the beginnings, this part of the New World was not a State of the Union. The people in those days remained close to the rivers. We have our roots then in the Arkansas River just as the Israelites with Moses as their leader found their roots in the Nile River.

    The State of Arkansas is preparing to celebrate its Sesquicentennial. For us, our beginnings are associated with Arkansas Post and the Church of St. Mary at Plum Bayou. Eventually, this part of the diocese became the Parish of St. Joseph in Pine Bluff.

    I am glad to write this letter and congratulate priests, religious and people who have been associated with the early roots of the Catholic Church in Arkansas, especially those who are currently members of St. Joseph's Parish, Pine Bluff. I commend you to the Lord. I praise you for the depth of your faith, the strength of your hope and the generosity of your love.

    I hope that readers will appreciate the history which is presented in this book. The people of St. Joseph's Parish can truly exclaim, "The Lord has been with us." It is my prayer that the Lord will remain with you for many years to come.

    Commending you to Mary the Mother of Jesus and the Mother of us all, and in a special way to St. Joseph, your patron, I remain,

                      Your friend,

                      +Andrew J. McDonald
                      Bishop of Little Rock

AJM/mmc

The Very Reverend Leo Anthony Riedmueller, V.F., Pastor of St. Joseph's Catholic Church.

My Dear Parishioners:

Saint Joseph's Parish has had a grand history. Many wonderful men and women have worked to make the Kingdom of God a reality in Pine Bluff. We salute these giants of faith, these dedicated and sacrificing people. The foundations of the parish were truly well laid, giving succeeding generations a solid structure of faith, hope, and charity upon which to build. We cannot single out each individual person. Only God knows the contributions each one has made. I truly believe that this is as it should be. And so, you will not find the names of everyone mentioned in this book. We can only touch the high points, limited as we are. We hold in fond memory those who have gone before us . . . we feel confident that they have attained their eternal reward . . . we only hope that we will be able to continue on the path they have so nobly left us. There is much that could be said and should be said. There are many who could say it more fittingly than I can. I acknowledge with humility the great work of the past accomplished by priests and laity. I am happy and grateful that I have the opportunity to be in St. Joseph's Parish at this time in history. I ask your prayers; I promise you mine. Proud of the past, confident of God's help, working together, the future of St. Joseph's will be glorious and fruitful.

In Christ,

Rev. Leo A. Riedmueller
Pastor

Preface

My association with St. Joseph's Parish, rather than any consciousness of literary ability, gave me hope that this writing might reveal something more of the spirit of this gracious section of the fine state of Arkansas.

This book is purposely informal and as a result is difficult to clarify. Perhaps the word *potpourri* might qualify, since the material is in turn narrative, genealogical and historical. It had its inception in the fulfillment of a promise to my pastor, Father Leo Riedmueller, that I would write the story of St. Joseph's Parish on the anniversary of our 125th year, and for the Sesquicentennial year of the State of Arkansas.

For years I have thought that it would be interesting to find within the covers of a single book, at least outlines of the Bishops of Arkansas, the Priests and families of St. Joseph's, and their environments down through the generations. Should some almost inevitable inaccuracies be found, I am truly sorry.

The material herein is largely documented, most of it having been secured from source material, court records, and letters. The gracious and generous response of living representatives made it possible to include many individuals who have been a part of this Parish. St. Joseph's Church takes pride in its many members who serve faithfully in professions, businesses, industry, local government, school systems and other occupations and at the same time, serving the Church. To these, and to all who have contributed data, I extend sincere thanks, and especially to Sister Catherine Markey, Archivist of the Diocese of Little Rock, Mr. Dave Wallis, our Honorable Mayor, Mr. Noel Bryant, a splendid attorney, Mr. C. Frank Williamson, my next door neighbor, Mr. John Webkes, my good friend and Mrs. Rowland Barthet, the world's greatest church secretary.

After many months of earnest and pleasurable preparation, this book is presented with the belief that it will be entertaining to the casual reader, helpful to the genealogist, and I hope, a source of pride in our Church History to the Parishioners of St. Joseph's, to whom it is affectionately dedicated.

E.R.L.

1984

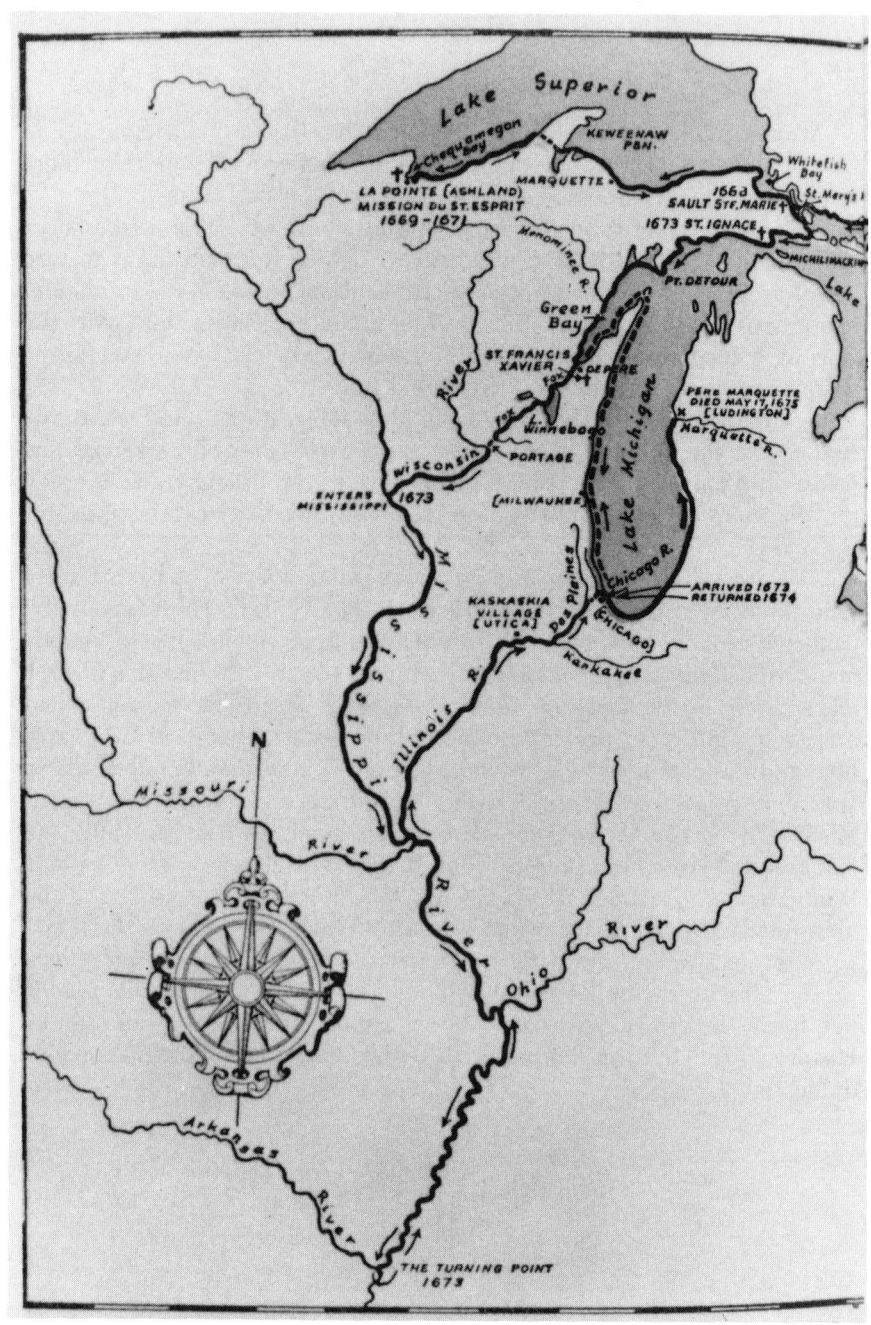

The Explorations of Père Marquette.

Chapter 1

Catholic Missionaries in Arkansas

It is sometimes difficult to realize beginnings, but let us turn back the stream of time, and look at our old and familiar places in the light of earlier days.

How many times when passing familiar landmarks, or walking along familiar streets have we not failed to see the many towns this town has been? And so it is in our County, our State and also our Church. Let us think backward and try to see these well known places through the eyes of the first European explorers and early Missionaries as they made their way through forests and over rivers, inhabited at that time by the native American Indian.

The history of the Catholic Church in Arkansas begins with the coming of the Spaniards in 1541. Sixty-six years before an English or French settlement was made in America, Hernando de Soto, with his band of conquistadores and missionaries, crossed the Mississippi River into the Arkansas country.[1]

The earliest settlement in Arkansas, in fact the earliest along the entire river line of the Mississippi, is Arkansas Post, on the Arkansas River, some twenty miles above its mouth. Where the Arkansas River joins the Mississippi, Father Jacques Marquette (1637–1675), and his men, in 1673 had turned their canoes northward, after having learned from the Indians that the river upon which they were navigating flowed into the Gulf of Mexico.[2]

One of the aims of Robert Cavalier Sieur de La Salle (1643–1687) and the French was to get control of the great waterways, in order to develop trade. To do this, the establishment of Posts was necessary, in order to have centers of control. With this in view, La Salle's Expedition was divided into two divisions: one led by Henri de Tonti, La Salle's faithful lieutenant, and Recollect missionary Father Zanobius Membre, who narrated the expedition.[3]

While in the Arkansas region, La Salle gave to Henri de Tonti, a seignorial grant,[4] and it was on this grant that the historic Arkansas Post was founded.[5]

De Tonti was evidently unable to give immediate attention to the development of the Arkansas concession, busied as he was with affairs at the Illinois post. No real establishment was made in the Arkansas country until de Tonti made his second voyage down the river in search of La Salle in 1686.[6]

In 1686, Henri de Tonti built a log house with a palisade, and there left six to ten men as a garrison, and as a beginning of a settlement.[7] The Quapaw Indians, once so numerous and powerful along the banks of the Red and Arkansas Rivers, after the erection of de Tonti's Fort, moved their principal village under its shadow. In 1687, after the assassination of La Salle, the party of Lt. Joutel, with Father John Cavalier, a Sulpician priest, and Father Douay, a Franciscan priest arrived at the fort on their return trip to Canada, and stayed[8] at Arkansas Post until August of 1787. It may be inferred that these priests exercised their sacerdotal functions and ministered to the French and Indians.[9]

On 26 November 1689, de Tonti gave a grant of land at Arkansas Post to the Jesuits of Fort St. Louis, Illinois, to establish a house and a chapel. He offered to pay for the support of the priest for the first three years. From that time on, Jesuits from the North visited Arkansas Post regularly. Father de Montigny, Father Davion, Father Charlevoix, the Jesuit historian in 1721, and Father Du Poisson who established a regular Indian Mission there. Father Cavette was the last of the Jesuit missionaries at the Post. In 1763, all of the Jesuits in Louisiana were banished by order of the Superior Council of Louisiana.[10]

Both the Fort and the adjoining settlement suffered heavily by the tremedous flood of 1763, and a new town was founded in 1764. The chapel of the Fort was dedicated to St. Stephen.[11]

In 1762 France ceded the Louisiana Territory west of the Mississippi to Spain. Thirty-seven years later, Spain ceded it back to France, and three years later the Louisiana Territory was incorporated into the United States.[12]

The veteran priest of the West was Father Pierre Gibault. Born Montreal, Canada, 7 April 1735, died New Madrid, Missouri, 15 August 1802.[13] This Father Gibault was the priest who played such a prominent part in the winning of the Northwest Territory for the United States. He gave invaluable aid to George Rogers Clark at Vincennes.[14]

During the Spanish regime, Arkansas Post may have been a canonical parish, several of the parish priests of St. Louis and Saint Genevieve served at the Post. Father Meurin, Father Guignes and Father Janin. The latter rebuilt the church of St. Stephen in 1796.[15]

The subscription list of the people at the Post consisted of the following names—Frederic Notrebene, James Lucas, Manuel Pertuis, Louis Placy, Rene Michel, Augustin Pinot, Antoine Pinot, Antoine Brinsback, Francois Daigle, Etienne Vasseur, Robert Brooks, Charles Bogy, John Pertuis, and two who are listed as Protestants—Hewes Scull and a Mr. Cummins.[16]

After Father Janin there were no more priests at the Post. Great overflows had caused the settlers to gradually move higher up the Arkansas River; the Fort was abandoned, and the Church of St. Stephen, wrecked. Still the Post continued to be the "Capital" of Arkansas Territory, until 1821, when Little Rock became the seat of the administration.[17]

The Reverend John Rosati, C.M., was consecrated coadjutor to Bishop Dubourg, 14 July 1820, and was especially entrusted with the care of Arkansas, Missouri and Western Illinois.[18]

Pope Leo VII divided the Diocese of Louisiana, 18 July 1826 and established the See of New Orleans, state of Louisiana as its diocese. All of the Louisiana Territory northward and west of the Mississippi was made the Diocese of St. Louis, with The Most Reverend John Rosati as Bishop. The diocese was estimated to contain at the most, 8000 Catholics. In 1843, the Diocese of Little Rock was established, embracing the State of Arkansas and the Indian Territory. The Most Reverend Andrew Byrne became the first Bishop.[19]

The first ordination was that of the Reverend Thomas McKeown, whom Bishop Byrne ordained at St. Ambrose Church, Arkansas Post, 1 November 1845.[20]

Chapter 2

St. Mary's Settlement and Cemetery Records

In the years 1820–1825, a new village was formed, a few miles from the old fort, higher up the river, by Hewes Scull, Louis Bogy, Robert McKay, Harold Stillwell and Isaac McLane.[1]

New faces began to appear along the Arkansas River, bringing with them the good and bad of civilization. One of the early settlers wrote:

"We are a motley crowd—good and bad, but bad seem to predominate."[2]

In order to learn of conditions in Arkansas, Bishop Rosati sent Father John Odin, and the Reverend Mr. John Timon, a sub-deacon, on a missionary journey in 1824.[3]

Father John Martin established a home and chapel in one of the settlements along the Arkansas River. Father Martin arrived at the Post in June, and after spending some time there, proceeded up the River. Father Martin did not succeed in his mission, and discouraged, returned to Louisiana.[4]

In the Fall of 1831, Bishop Rosati sent Father Edmund Saulnier, and the newly ordained Father Pierre Beauprez to the wilderness of Arkansas. They arrived at the Post in December and found neither house nor chapel.[5]

In the meantime, Father Beauprez had gone up the river, and here he found 38 Catholic families—16 of them located 18 miles below Pine Bluff (at New Gascony), and 22 at the village.[6]

These people could very easily have built a church and supported a priest, but difficulty arose concerning the location of the church. New Gascony wanted the church near them, while the others wanted it at Pine Bluff. Due to the great rivalry between the two groups, Father Beauprez made little progress in uniting the Catholics into one church.[7]

Father Saulnier's health was bad, and he returned to St. Louis. Father Beauprez, discouraged over the split factions of Jefferson County, wrote Bishop Rosati, 12 July 1832:[8]

> "The departure of my confrere, Mr. Saulnier, afflicts and discourages me much. I do not think I shall see him again. Here I am in this wretched country, abandoned, alone! With tears in my eyes, I have wished a hundred times that I had never heard mention of America, never had seen it. In Europe, in my own country, I could have saved my soul; but here, there is much to fear. But Father, for the love of my salvation, have pity on me! Take me from this suburb of Hell!
> Your obedient and faithful servant,
> P. F. Beauprez
> Unworthy priest"[9]

Bishop Rosati took pity on Father Beauprez, and appointed him to Apple Creek.[10] (Apple Creek was a mission in Perry County, Missouri where the knowledge of German was needed; Father Beauprez spoke some German.)

For the third time, Bishop Rosati made an effort to establish the Catholic Church in Arkansas. He appointed Father Annemond Dupuy, a stout hearted Frenchman, to the Post.[12]

In writing the Bishop, Father Dupuy said:

"I have now talked to a great number of the inhabitants (of the Post). It seems they are not particularly anxious to have a church and priest. You see, Monseigneur, that this is not very encouraging. Do not give credence to the report that Saulnier and Beauprez have exaggerated; no, what they said is but too true. Everything here is excessively dear. I have already spent fifty dollars and suffered much. I see but too well that all I shall have to endure surpasses my strength; but no matter; I left my country with the firm resolution to lay down my life, if necessary. I went away from St. Louis convinced that I was going to death; so I shall carry out my resolutions; I shall conquer or die for the Name of Jesus and of the Blessed Virgin Mary, from whom I expect all, my help and my reward. Tomorrow I shall start for Pine Bluff, seventy miles from here."[13]

Father Dupuy did come to Pine Bluff, where he fixed his residence in the log mission opened by Father Beauprez below the village.[14] He wrote to Bishop Rosati:

"12 November 1832
I have made the journey to Pine Bluff; I found there much better

dispositions than at the Post. The people are much more simple, more religious, and less arrogant. Conditions for a religious center are better there. There is no Congress land,[15] neither at the Post, nor at Pine Bluff, fit for a settlement. At the Post there is none even for sale except at an exorbitant price, ten dollars an acre, and poor soil at that. The people of Pine Bluff, which is a village of about 50 families, Catholic and Protestant, scattered over the space of 12 miles, are less prejudiced against religion and its ministers—although a certain individual has raked me over the coals... he passed in review all the missionaries who ever came to this country... and finished by belching forth all sorts of insults against the priests in general, saying that he would not permit one of them to put his foot in his backyard, and mark well, Monseigneur, that I was right then in the accursed backyard......."[16]

Father Dupuy was made of other stuff than Father Saulnier and Father Beauprez; he swallowed these bitter pills, and held out. He bought ten arpents[17] of ground from Mr. Vaugine, three miles below Pine Bluff near a cemetery which eight years before had been blessed by Father Odin.[18]

By the Spring of 1833, Father Dupuy began to see the results of his labor. He won the trust of the people and succeeded in having them attend Mass and receive the Sacraments frequently. Not only was the Pine Bluff congregation responding to the appeals of Father Dupuy, but also the Catholics below the village.[19]

In 1834, Father Dupuy fell ill with "bilious fever" from which he recovered, however, it was soon apparent that he would need assistance. This resulted in the appointment of Father Peter Donnelly.[20]

On 6 April 1837, Father Dupuy wrote the Bishop a letter which is interesting because it contains some statistical items: "The number of Catholics, nominal and others, does not go beyond six hundred; they are scattered in the four corners of the state. Most of them are in Jefferson County; then follows the Post in Arkansas County, then Little Rock and surroundings".......... "there are four places where Mass might be said, if we had the money to travel, by using the cabins in which the settlers live. (1) Three miles below Pine Bluff(s), which is the seat of justice for Jefferson County; on the left river bank is the chapel and the priest's house which I built. (2) At New Gascony, fifteen miles lower down and in the same county, fifteen families could be gathered if Mass were celebrated there. (3) At Arkansas Post, sixty miles from my chapel; but there is no chapel, and it is so difficult to build one, because the people do not pull together"....... "(4) at Petit Rocher (Little Rock); but just a chapel must be built there........"[21]

Father Dupuy and Father Donnelly apparently did not get along too well. Father Dupuy wrote to Bishop Rosati concerning a school which his communicants were requesting: "As far as the school goes (in his own mission), I am afraid I cannot have it, because neither at St. Louis nor at New Orleans, could I raise enough to pay a teacher. Mr. Donnelly is not capable to teach what is required, because he cannot write his own language correctly; besides his health is poor".[22]

Bishop Rosati transferred Father Dupuy to New Orleans and appointed Father Donnelly pastor of the Arkansas missions. Thus the builder of St. Mary's left the state, hurt and heartbroken. His departure left the Catholics of Jefferson County in split factions. One led by John Dodge opposed Father Donnelly, while the other faction, led by Antoine Barraque, stood by Father Donnelly.[23]

Father Donnelly supervised the building of the first Catholic School in Arkansas . . . St. Mary's Academy. The school under the direction of Mother Agnes Hart, of the Sisters of Loretto, Loretto, Kentucky, opened in 1838.[24] An article which appeared in the Arkansas Gazette 14 November 1983 listed the terms of the school as follows:

"Boarding, per annum $104. Tuition in common branches including orthography, reading, writing, grammar, arithmetic and geography, plain sewing and marking, per annum, $24. French language, extra per annum, $20. History, natural philosophy, chemistry and the use of globes, fancy and bead work, per annum, $20. Music, with use of piano, per annum, $40."

"Washing, per annum $18, bedding if furnished by institution, $8. A bed stead and mosquito bar can be furnished per annum for $2. Doctor's fees, medicine, etc. per annum $8."[25] (Ah! the "Good Old Days!")

From the copy of the original account book of old St. Mary's Academy, the following list of pupils from 1838 to 1844 was taken:

PUPILS	PARENT OR GUARDIAN
Elizabeth & Eulalia Taylor	Creed Taylor
Samuel Taylor	Creed Taylor
B. Lee	F. Lee
Louise Dodge	John Dodge
Huldah & Isabelle Rigney	W. Rigney
Celestine, Louisine & Celise Vaugine	F. N. Vaugine
Mary & Frances Roane	Judge Samuel C. Roane
Benjamin & James Vaugine	F. N. Vaugine
"His little daughter"	Paul Vaugine
Elizabeth Brooks	Robert Brooks
Theresa, Jane & Janette Derreseaux	Paul Derreseaux
Andrew Derreseaux	Paul Derreseaux
Mary & Frances Vallier	Francis Vallier
Frances, Hiacinthe & Georginia Tenas	R. Tenas
Elizabeth Pertuis	M. Pertuis

19

PUPILS	PARENT OR GUARDIAN
Ataline & Matilda Bogy	F. Bogy
Miss Young (10 days)	Mr. Young
"Children of Mr. Hibert"	Mr. Hibert
Ann Maria Scull	James Scull
Frances Scull (niece)	James Scull
Mary Bramber	R. Bramber
Nancy & Adeline Farrelly	C. F. Farrelly
Caroline Dugan	Mr. Dugan
Amand & Teresia McCann	F. McCann
Malelda Bogy	L. Bogy
Nancy Dagle	L. Bogy
Eugenia E. Buck	James Buck
Miss McGuire	J. McGuire
———Greenfield	T. G. Greenfield
Mary Dickerson	T. Dickerson
Alcinda & Lucinda Simpson	J. Simpson
Frances & Cornelia Simpson (orphan daughters of Thompson Simpson & Frances Fairfax)	J. Simpson
Mary & Emily Washington	C. Washington
Clemence Brooks	Mrs. Paulite
Matilda Watson	George Watson
Miss Cammick (niece)	George Watson
Agnes Bord	George Watson
Martha Ann Hibbard	John Hibbard
Elizabeth Piere Mitchell	Piere Mitchell
Evaline Downing	David Maxwell
James Malpose	John Malpose
Miss Reeder	Thomas Reeder[26]

Four years later, St. Mary's Academy was moved to Arkansas Post, where it was known as St. Ambrose Academy.[27]

In 1843, the Diocese of Little Rock was established; the French priests left and Bishop Byrne and Irish priests arrived. Sometime between 1839 and 1851, the site of St. Mary's was moved to its present location on Plum Bayou.[28]

Before we leave the early Catholic settlements along the Arkansas River, mention should be made of the Quapaw Indian who figures prominently in the final decades of the tribe in Arkansas. That Quapaw Indian was Saracen, born about 1735. Saracen is listed in the Quapaw Treaty of 1824 as a half breed Quapaw. His father is believed to be Cadet Francois Sarazin.[29]

Saracen is best known as the Rescuer of Captive Children. The commonly accepted version today is the rescue of the settler's two children who were stolen by a band of Chickasaw Indians.[30]

In 1829, Saracen, then over 90 years old, feeling that death was not far off, journeyed from the Quapaw reservation in the Indian Territory to Little Rock, and begged Governor John Pope to permit him to die on his old hunting ground near Pine Bluff. His request was granted. The Lazarist missionaries, in 1824 had erected an altar before the wigwam of Saracen, who received them very kindly.[31]

A mutual friendship was thus formed, and in 1888, in commemoration of Saracen, a memorial window in his honor was placed in St. Joseph's Church.[32]

Saracen's body was first interred about 1832 in the Pine Bluff Cemetery (old), located then between 3rd and 4th Avenues and Chestnut and Pine Streets. Father Lucey was responsible for marking the grave of Saracen.... on 13 May 1887, Father Lucey wrote Bishop Fitzgerald stating that Saracen was buried about 50 years previously in the old town cemetery back of the Methodist Church at 4th and Main. Father Lucey doubted that Saracen was a Catholic, but accepted the opinion of Judge Bocage that he was.[33] Consequently Father Lucey asked the Bishop's permission to move the body of Saracen to St. Joseph's Cemetery.[34]

Chapter 3

St. Mary's, Plum Bayou and Cemetery Records

Originally, St. Mary's was located on Boyd's Point, north of Pine Bluff. The Point began at the old Free Bridge site, as the river ran south, then it turned and ran north for an equal distance until it made another bend which is known as Ste. Marie. Years ago, the river on the west side of the Point began meandering east, so the church was moved some three and one half miles northeast on Plum Bayou, ca. 1839–51—its present location.[1]

With St. Mary's even further from Pine Bluff and with the establishment of St. Joseph's in Pine Bluff, the old church began to wane in influence. Today, it is like the parent, grown old and being cared for by the child.[2]

Mrs. Emma F. Vaugine White's place of birth was St. Mary's landing on the Arkansas River. In 1927, she obtained permission from Bishop Morris to restore and preserve St. Mary's Church and Cemetery on Plum Bayou, as a memorial to her son, Allen White. In her last will and testament, Mrs. White made St. Mary's Church and Cemetery, Plum Bayou, the sole beneficiary of her estate, to provide for the perpetual care of the historic shrine.[3]

In March of 1974, the Arkansas Historic Preservation Committee approved the nomination of St. Mary's, Plum Bayou to the National Register of Historic Places. After much correspondence, the United States Department of Interior wrote in October of 1974: "After careful consideration, we are returning the nomination for St. Mary's Catholic Church, because in our opinion it has not maintained sufficient historical integrity to merit listing on the National Register. As you mentioned in the nomination, the 1927 remodeling destroyed most of the buildings' architectural significance."[4]

St. Mary's is under the administration of St. Joseph's, with Mass being

St. Mary's Church, Plum Bayou, before restoration. Photograph, courtesy of Lites-Wallis Collection.

St. Mary's Church, Plum Bayou, after restoration. Photograph, courtesy of Mr. John Webkes.

Bell in tower of St. Mary's Church, Plum Bayou. Photograph, courtesy of Mr. John Webkes.

held in the old church only on special occasions.

For those scholars who would delve further into the records of this particular area, it is recommended that the French records of 1831–1853 be searched.[5]

CEMETERY RECORDS OF ST. MARY'S

Mrs. M. T. Alcorn, born 17 May 1843, died 18 January 1878
Mrs. Antwine, died 1874
Teresa Bogy, died 1875
James Brooks, no dates
Mary C. Brooks, born about 1806, died 25 March 1857
Robert Brooks, died 25 December 1857

Cemetery—St. Mary's Church, Plum Bayou. Photograph, courtesy of Mr. John Webkes.

William Brooks, born 4 May 1825, died 7 October 1876
Adell Burton, no dates
R. M. Burton, born Wilson County, Tennessee 1837, died 4 June 1879
Sydney Burton, no dates
Virginia Burton, died 1869
Mrs. Virginia Cobbs, born 6 April 1855, died 17 December 1911
Mike Collins, born New Orleans, Louisiana, died 9 October 1884
Mrs. Sam Coosotte, died 1876
Mrs. Dabb, no dates
Margaret Dardanne, born about 1866, died 1867
Francis T. Davis, born 11 February 1873, died 9 February 1901
Mrs. Dechase, died 1872
Mrs. Mary E. Dent, born 1 September 1833, Charles County, Md., died 15 February 1857
Alice Derreuisseaux, no dates
Audile Derreuisseaux, Infant
Cecilia Derreuisseaux, died 30 July 1859
Eleanor Derreuisseaux, born 11 January 1855, died 23 August 1859
Elizabeth Derreuisseaux, born 13 May 1831, died 9 January 1871
Cecilia Derreuisseaux, born 13 April 1850, died 15 March 1852
Frances B. Derreuisseaux, born 31 March 1865, died 8 November 1891
Frankie X. Derreuisseaux, born 26 October 1820, died 18 March 1894
Mrs. Joe Derreuisseaux, born 2 February 1853, died 12 February 1893

John B. Derreuisseaux, born 13 June 1849, died 22 March 1852
Hypolite Derreuisseaux, no dates
Lulie A. Derreuisseaux, born 26 May 1857, died 9 August 1859
Robert Deshay, no dates
Mrs. Ann Diamond, died 14 October 1892
John W. Diamond, born 8 October 1860, died 2 January 1904
Joseph Diamond, no dates
W. M. Diamond, died 1865
Annie Louise Donelson, born 1882, died 15 August 1883
Andrew George Dugan, no dates
Caroline Dugan, no dates
Noble Dugan, died 1875
Petronella Dugan, no dates
Richard N. Dugan, born 11 July 1818, died 25 July 1860
Emily Foley, died 15 November 1864
John Foley, born 1812, died 1879
Michael Foley, died 15 November 1850
Missoria Foley, died 15 January 1875
Patrick Foley, died 15 November 1871
Thomas Foley, died 1860
Elizabeth Jane George, born 13 March 1823, died 9 October 1884
Mother Agnes Hart, Mother Superior of Convent at Scull Place, died April 1841
Catherine L. Henton, born 6 April 1860, died 11 August 1863
Lula L. Henton, born 6 January 1862, died 31 August 1863
Phillip H. Henton, born 7 January 1870, died 2 November 1872
——Holcombe, no dates
Jane Hudgens, born April 1821, died 2 July 1863
Deliah Jenkins, born 21 August 1863, died 16 December 1885
Francis N. Jenkins, born 16 March 1849, died 10 July 1867
H. Jenkins, born 20 March 1851, died about 1868
Mary L. Jenkins, born 6 November 1827, died 24 July 1866
Mattie Mayfield, died 29 April 1891
Mrs. Fanny Mitchell, no dates
Frank Mitchell, born 22 July 1838, died 1848
J. C. Mitchell, born 25 December 1847, died 30 July 1912
J. M. Mitchell, born 7 March 1843
John Mitchell, no dates
John B. Mitchell, Jr., born 11 February 1840
John B. Mitchell, Sr., born 14 November 1815, died about 1848
Louis Mitchell, born 29 November 1862, died 10 March 1911
Peter Mitchell, no dates
Hugh Murray, died about 1863

Henry McNeal, died 1875
Patrick O'Connell, died 7 June 1875
Elnora Patton, died 1854—infant
Mary C. Patton, born 1827, died 1865
Mrs. Peter, born 1819, died 6 October 1893
Sister Wallis, died 1869
Mrs. Sullivan, died 1873
Unnamed, died 26 August 1859
Agnes B. Vaugine, born 16 April 1876, died 16 May 1895
Audile Vaugine, born 10 March 1808, died 4 October 1876
Catherine O. Vaugine, born 17 December 1837, died 22 January 1867
Charles I. Vaugine, born 29 August 1829, died 5 September 1836
Elizabeth Vaugine, aged about 35, 1875
Grandmother Vaugine, died about 1817
Grandfather Vaugine, born 6 August 1768, died May 1831
Francis N. Vaugine, died 26 August 1859
Frank G. Vaugine, born 13 July 1831, died 7 July 1900
F. N. Vaugine, born 31 May 1800, died 26 January 1846
Mrs. Mary Vaugine, died 23 March 1852
Mary E. Vaugine, born 17 December 1844, died 27 November 1869
Monet Vaugine, no dates
M. T. R. Vaugine, born 9 February 1841, died May 1865
Paul Vaugine, no dates
Phillip N. Vaugine, born 24 February 1836, died 8 March 1900
Stephen Vaugine, born 28 December 1833, died 28 July 1839
F. D. Vallier, born 1 August 1823, died 17 April 1866
Joseph W. Value, born 30 October 1831, died 10 March 1861
Mary Value, died 29 September 1891
Mollie Marshall Whitley, born 5 March 1876, died 10 October 1908

Chapter 4

St. Peter's, New Gascony and Cemetery Records

Old St. Peter's Catholic cemetery, about a mile south of the present Altheimer—Reydel road, is all that is left to remind present day visitors of old New Gascony.[1]

At one time, New Gascony was an important landing on the river, and was briefly the seat of the county government, but then gradually drifted into oblivion.[2]

Undoubtedly, Antoine Barraque originally settled the site. G. W. Featherstonhaugh, the English traveler and geologist, met Antoine Barraque as he went down the river in December in 1835. Mr. Featherstonhaugh wrote of Antoine Barraque in his book, "Excursion Through the Slave States," published at London in 1844:[3] "He (Barraque) is now a successful cotton planter and being himself a native of the lower Pyrenees, has given the name New Gascony to the district he resides in."[4]

Ten years later, Antoine Barraque was definitely at New Gascony and was quite an influence in its behalf. He wanted to move the county government there, and did accomplish the move for a short period of time. He also wanted the Catholic Church to centralize its operation at New Gascony, which resulted in a split among Catholics in the county.[5]

Bishop Rosati settled the issue in favor of the Pine Bluff church. The county seat was moved back to Pine Bluff and Antoine Barraque moved up the river in the vicinity of old Red Bluff, east of the present day town of Redfield. Antoine Barraque died at the home of a son-in-law, B. F. Smith in Pine Bluff, 29 October 1858.[6]

For those readers who might desire further genealogical information concerning St. Peter's Church, New Gascony, a baptismal register may be found in the Grand Prairie Historical Society Bulletin, Volume 25, Nos. 3 and 4.

New Gascony became a peaceful farming community, its tranquility shattered only during the Brooks-Baxter war when that war's only skirmish was fought there.[7]

Creed Taylor settled in the locality of New Gascony in the early 1840's.[8] According to the papers "The Arkansas Mission Under Rosati," compiled by the Reverend F. G. Holweck, Creed Taylor was one of the principal benefactors when the Sisters of Loretto opened the school at St. Mary's.[9] Father Donnelly wrote: "Their principal benefactor was Mr. Creed Taylor, a convert who had been baptized by Father Dupuy."[10]

Early Interments: New Gascony Cemetery—St. Peter's Church Yard[11]

Bradshaw—Theodosia Malvina, died 16 May 1859, aged 41 years, 10 months and 29 days (consort of W. H. Bradshaw)

Caulk—Maggie E. (Taylor), died 23 October 1881, aged 18 years, 11 months and 23 days (wife of S. V. Caulk)

_____, born St. Clair County, Illinois, 3 January 1803 and died 14 October 1871, Jefferson County, Arkansas

Dardenne—America G., September 1848–12 July 1852

Dardenne—Stanislaus, born November 1809, died 19 April 1854

Dodge—Etiennette, died 30 March 1847, aged 51 years, 6 months and 20 days

Dodge—John, died 9 July 1845, aged 49 years, 6 months and 2 days

Gocio—Emily, 19 November 1843, 11 October 1859 (daughter of Louis and Emily Gocio)

Gocio—Joseph, 7 May 1837, died 25 October 1854

Gracie—Robert, died 4 December 1853, aged 2 years, 3 months and 19 days (son of P. B. and A. E. Gracie)

Moore—"Underneath sleep(s) the remains of *Mrs. Julia S. Moore*, who died in Napoleon, Arkansas, 16 May 1859, aged about 32 years. Erected to her memeory by her affectionate husband, Joseph S. Moore of Napoleon, Arkansas."

Murphy

    Francis D., died 19 November 1858, aged 3 years

    James and *Walter C.*, who died in infancey—children of Matthew and Fanny Murphy

Pinot

    Amelia A., died 2 May 1859, aged 55 years (wife of Peter)

    Emelia E., born 24 September 1836, died 13 July 1855

Scull

Louisa, born 8 August 1821, died 2 September 1845 (wife of James Scull)

John C. Jones, born 20 November 1841, died 20 September 1844, son of James Scull and wife Louisa

Mary Louisa, born 21 June 1843, died 21 July 1846 (daughter of James Scull and wife Louisa)

Taylor

Ann C., died 27 May 1855, aged 18 years and 2 months (wife of S. C. Taylor)

Creed, born 10 January 1800, died 8 June 1887

Eulalie, died 1 August 1827 (wife of Creed Taylor)

Mary (Boone), 15 January 1801, died 12 July 1879 (wife of Creed Taylor)

Samuel C., born 23 October 1881, died 23 August 1888 (son of Z. and N. P. Taylor)

Mary Ann (Valliere), died 9 November 1837, in the 36th year of her age (wife of Creed Taylor)

Chapter 5
Old French Cemetery

Located in the West Half of the Southeast Quarter, Section 34, Township 5 South, Range 9 West—Commonly known as the Valliere Reserve. Jefferson County deeds disclose that this land was owned and resided upon by Joseph Bonne, Sr., (reputed to have been the first white settler of Pine Bluff), for thirty years up to and including the time of his death in April 1860. Such records further reveal that at the time of death of Joseph Bonne, Sr., a cemetery existed in such property.[1]

It should be noted that the grant of Francis Coussot (in the Quapaw Treaty) adjoined the Valliere grant on the East, and that Joseph Bonne, Sr., about 1830, sold the eighty acres granted to him (Joseph Bonne, Sr.) to Antoine Barraque, and at the same time, purchased the Valliere eighty acres from him, Barraque having previously acquired the tract from the original grantee, Joseph Valliere.[2]

A cemetery project was undertaken primarily in the hope of locating a marker for Joseph Bonne, Sr., if one existed.[3]

Markers for the following persons were unearthed:
1. *Thomas Nathan* born 3 March 1857, died 12 August 1858, aged 1 year, 5 months and 9 days
    Caroline Lutecia born 26 October 1851, died 24 September 1858, aged 6 years, 10 months and 24 days (son and daughter of N. H. and E. L. Cloyes)
2. *Stephen,* son of P. and C. Coosotte, born 20 September 1852, died 25 January 1853
3. *Margaret,* daughter of P. and F. Coosotte, born 8 October 1841, died 1 October 1849
4. *Joseph Francis,* son of P. and C. Coosotte, born 9 January 1856, died 22 April 1857

31

5. Small marker, a fragment bearing only the initials "M. C."
6. *Felicity Coosotte,* died 24 January 1849, aged 27 years.[4]

Joe Davis Neal, of 2318 East Pullen Street, who lived in sight of this cemetery for all of his 72 years, stated that it was known locally as "The Old French Cemetery," and that he knew of no one being buried there during his life time. His sister, Laura Humphrey of 2313 East Barraque Street, aged 89 told him that when she was a little girl, some bodies from this cemetery had been exhumed and reinterred in St. Joseph's Catholic Cemetery in Pine Bluff. Efforts to verify this occurrence in the records of St. Joseph's cemetery proved unavailing.[5]

Chapter 6

Early Catholic Families

Joseph Bonne Of Joseph Bonne's lineage, the first in America was probably a restless, thrifty Frenchman who left his mother country, found only disappointment in his chosen St. Lawrence River colony, and followed the path made by the earlier French explorers, Jesuit priests and missionaries. He, with others, sought a home southward in a warmer climate, where rumor promised fertile land for the taking, along the rivers.[1]

La Salle had blazed the trail for these home seekers and had appointed de Tonti and ten men in 1686, to make a white settlement in the lower river country to be designated, Arkansas Post.[2]

Several of these "ten men" left with de Tonti, took young Indian squaws and "married them when next the Missionary Padres came along." One of these ten Frenchmen was probably the first Bonne in Arkansas—perhaps in America.[3]

It is known that Joseph Bonne was born in 1793—his mother, a Quapaw Indian, and that he was baptized by a Padre of his father's Catholic faith.[4]

Available 1801 records show that "fifty miles up the Arkansas River on Bonne Reserve, lived Joseph Bonne, Michael Bonne and other tax-payers named Bonne."[5] Joseph Bonne married Mary Imbeau, daughter of Francois Imbeau and lived in New Gascony, and it was there that Joseph Bonne in 1818–1819, as an interpreter for the United States Government, signed the Quapaw Treaty.

When the Arkansas River flooded New Gascony in 1819, Joseph Bonne sought land on the south bank of the river, about five miles above St. Mary's Catholic Church. He probably began building a log cabin home for his family, as they were with him before winter arrived.

33

Antoine Barraque

In the home of Joseph Bonne were held the first Jefferson County and probate sessions and records reveal that all sessions of the courts were held in the home of Joseph Bonne, until a log court house was built on Court Square, facing Pullen Street.

Antoine Barraque Much has been written over the years about Antoine Barraque . . . and yet a few questions linger. For example, where and when did Monsieur Barraque enter the United States? Where and when did he marry Mary Therese Dardenne? Some doubts seems to exist as to the correct answers.[6]

G. W. Featherstonhaugh, on the subject of Antoine Barraque's marriage said simply:

"Frenchmen make a point of never being unhappy long, so he married the daughter of one of the settlers at whose home he stayed; after a while, with the assistance of his father-in-law, he built a house and cleared a plantation."[7]

Antoine Barraque died in 1858 at the Pine Bluff home of his son-in-law,

Benjamin Franklin Smith.[8]

It is puzzling, how Antoine Barraque, who only arrived in Arkansas in 1816, became so proficient in the Indian language, that he was able to serve as interpreter in the 1824 treaty with the Quapaws, and as an Indian sub-agent for the United States government. When it is remembered that the Quapaws had no alphabet nor written language, the accomplishment seems even greater in such a short period.[9]

Antoine Barraque had married Mary Therese Dardenne ... and in some baptismal records of Arkansas Post, was that the mother of Mary Therese Dardenne was a full-blooded Indian. Antoine Barraque had lived at the Dardenne home before his marriage. The Indian tongue was doubtless spoken in their home on a daily basis by all members, and so Antoine Barraque had the best of tutors.[10]

Antoine Barraque was an educated man who knew Latin enough to write a letter in Latin. He entirely neglected his religion, but during the regime of Father Dupuy, together with Frederic Notrebene, the "Atheist" of the Post (Arkansas Post), returned to the practice of the Catholic religion.[11]

Joseph Valliere and the Vaugine Family Arkansas County records show that Don Joseph Valliere was in command of the Post of Arkansas in 1787. In 1793 in acknowledgement of Don Joseph Valliere's services, Baron de Carondelet, Governor of Louisiana made him a land grant which made up a tract of over 6,000,000 acres and on the map of today, includes, Ozark, Douglas, Stone, Barry, Christian and Taney counties in Missouri, and about a dozen counties in Arkansas, making a tract 80 miles wide, and 120 miles broad. When Joseph Valliere died sometime in 1799, he possessed "of the largest lot of real estate ever owned by a royal subject." No move was made for a complete title after his death and later Louisiana was transferred from Spain to France, and then in 1803 to the United States.[12]

Although the grant was legally made, according to Spanish customs of that period, the land was situated in a region inhabited and surrounded by hostile Indian tribes, which prevented the establishment of a settlement.[13]

In 1845 Joseph Valliere's heirs brought suit to recover the land, but the case was decided against them in 1847, on the grounds that the grantee had failed to carry out the provisions regarding settlement, occupation and improvement.[14]

Joseph Valliere married Marie Felicite de Moran about 1763, a native of New Orleans, and had four children prior to his arrival in the District of Arkansas. The oldest, Bernard, second Marie Felicite, Francois, and Eugenia. Joseph Valliere reached Arkansas Post some time in the early part of 1787. Bernard and Eugenia had probably died, as no mention is made of

Don Joseph Bernard Valliere D'Hauterive

them in the Arkansas records, but there was another daughter, her name given as Augustine, Elizabeth Augustine or Marie Augustine. She married Louis Jordelas, whose parents were from New Orleans, and disappears from church and family records.[15] Marie Felicite Valliere married Francois Nuisement de Vaugine, and their children's names are interesting to us as we develop this history, because as noted in other segments of this work, these names are so intertwined with the early settlers of this region.

The children of Francois Vaugine and his wife, Marie Felicite Valliere were:

Manette Vaugine who married James Scull

Eulalie Vaugine who married Creed Taylor in October 1821 and died in August 1827.

Francois Vaugine born 1800 married Audile Desruisseaux

Etienne Vaugine who married Mathilde Desruisseaux

Etienette Vaugine who married John Dodge

Paul Vaugine who married Harriet Wolfe

Two sons of Francois Vaugine married two daughters of his second wife, and this caused a double relationship between the Vaugine and Bogy families. Francois Vaugine's daughter, Manette (see above) married James Scull, and his brother, Hewes, married a sister of Mrs. Mary Vaugine, second wife of Francois Vaugine. Another sister, Catherine Bogy married Don Carlos de Villmont, a former Commandant of Arkansas Post, and by these and other marriages, the Valliere-Vaugine family became allied with the most influential families living in Arkansas District.[16] In St. Joseph's Parish today, we still have descendants of the Valliere-Vaugine families.

John Noble was born 3 June 1778 in Tennessee, son of Marco Noble and Cathalena Hellet. John Noble was baptized by Father Janin, 11 May 1779 in Arkansas. His grandparents were Juan Noble and Elizabeth Carle, and great grandparents, Jacoba Noble and Mackerly Carola.[17]

In 1827 John Noble married Frances Gravier, born 1807 in Arkansas. On 12 August 1836, John Noble purchased 80 acres of land from Alexander Stephens, and in September of 1842 he paid $1.25 per acre for an additional 160 acres of land. In all he owned 240 acres in or about the South half of the Northeast quarter of Section 25, Township Number 6 South, Range number 8 West.[18] It will be noted later in this text, that St. Paul's Church, Noble Lake, Arkansas bears in its deed, the adjoining Range and Section lines as the land described as belonging to John Noble in 1836.

Prior to 1830, John Noble helped with the building of St. Peter's Church, New Gascony. He has many descendants in Pine Bluff and several counties in Arkansas.[19]

Creed Taylor One of the most active layman of St. Mary's Parish, and afterwards of St. Peter's at New Gascony from 1836 to 1887. Creed Taylor was born near Harrodsburg, Kentucky, 10 January 1800, and came to Arkansas in 1819. He was married 22 October 1821 by John Dodge, to Eulalie Vaugine, granddaughter of the Spanish Governor, Joseph Valliere,[20] and daughter of Francois Vaugine. Creed Taylor was a convert to the Catholic Church in 1836.[21] He was the first territorial sheriff in Jefferson County and when Arkansas was admitted to the Union, he was elected the first county judge.[22]

Eulalie Vaugine Taylor died 1 August 1827, and Creed Taylor married the second time, August 1828, Marie Ann Valliere, also a granddaughter of Joseph Valliere and a cousin of his first wife. Marie Ann Valliere died 9 November 1837, and on 15 November 1838, Creed Taylor married Mary C. Boone, who died 12 July 1879.[23] Creed Taylor is quoted as saying in regard to hardships endured by pioneers to this region:

"I look backward to those days with pleasure, as I believe that there was more genuine hospitality, truer friendship and real honesty in the land than anywhere exists today." "I am an old man now, and life's evening shadows

Mr. Creed Taylor. Photograph from a sketch by Jon Kennedy.

are beginning to fall, yet I shall never regret coming to this State, or the struggles encountered here to establish a home."[24]

Creed Taylor died 8 June 1887, and is buried in St. Peter's Cemetery at New Gascony.

James Scull If one studies the history of Jefferson County, sooner or later he will encounter James Scull. He was the first Postmaster (of Jefferson County) and was Territorial Treasurer for a number of years. In the Trimble Collection in the Arkansas History Commission are two letters, handwritten by James Scull to his friend James Miller, first Territorial Governor of Arkansas. In these letters, James Scull tells of his intention of moving to Jefferson County, and eventually he did so, settling at Boyd's Point.[25] James Scull was married to Manette Vaugine, the sister of Creed Taylor's wife, aforementioned.

Stanislaus Dardenne was born November 1809, died 19 April 1854, buried at St. Peter's Cemetery, New Gascony.[26] Stanislaus Dardenne was the first sheriff of Jefferson County under the state administration. He knew his duty and did it well. A native Frenchman, his name was given to Dardenne Street, now known as Alabama.[27] (Names of streets in Pine Bluff were changed in the 1880's.)

John Dodge was the first Postmaster in what is now Jefferson County. He was appointed Postmaster at Vaugine, 27 April 1825. Vaugine was in the vicinity of New Gascony and John Dodge is buried at St. Peter's Catholic Cemetery at New Gascony.[28] He married Etienette Vaugine.

Other prominent early Catholic families were: Ignatius Bogy, Baptiste Soire, Baptiste Bonne, Lewis Bartholomew, Antoine Duchassin, Baptiste Imbeau, and Francis Coupot.

Chapter 7

St. Joseph's Church, Pullen and Georgia Streets

Today it is easy to confuse the early sites of two Pine Bluff churches. Lot one in block 13 was purchased by Peter German and James C. Groce for the First Methodist Church. (Deed Book B. I, p. 138—Jefferson County Court House). The Catholic Church purchased Lot four, in block 13, on 7 July 1838. (Deed Book B, p. 246, Jefferson County Court House.)[1]

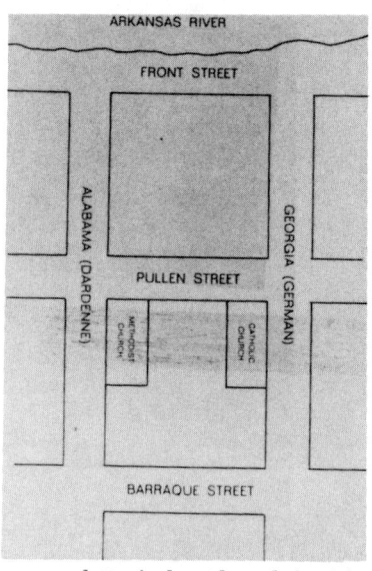

Location of the second Catholic Church building in Pine Bluff.

The second St. Joseph's Catholic Church building, circa 1868. Photograph, courtesy of Mr. John Webkes.

The accompanying map will show the location of Pine Bluff's second Catholic Church. The shaded areas of the map represent the present Lake Pine Bluff and the north (Martha Mitchell) Expressway as we know it today.[2]

There is great uncertainty as to when this first church was built. Monsignor Lucey's Handbook of St. Joseph's Church of 1907 says:

"Mass was said fifty years ago (1857) for some length of time in a log house where the Citizen's Bank now stands." This house was owned by the Scull family. He further says:

"In the course of time, a frame church building was erected on East Pullen Street near the present steamboat wharf." The intimation would seem to be that the first church (on this site) was built about the year 1858 or 1859.[3]

However, it should be noted that the deed to the property at Pullen and Georgia Streets, states:

"This indenture made and entered into this 7th day of *July 1838* between Anthony H. Davis, James J. Chowning, William M. Pincard, and Henry S. Dawson proprietors and owners of the Town of Pine Bluff... on the first part, and Joseph Rosati, Bishop of St. Louis on the second part..."

According to Diocesan records, a permanent pastor was appointed in the year 1858. The baptismal and other records actually on hand in St. Joseph's Church today begin in the year 1858. The Reverend P. I. Clarke

From Jefferson County, Arkansas-----Deed Book B, Page 246.

This indenture made and entered into this 7th day of July 1838 by and between Anthony H. Davis, James J. Chowning, William M. Pincard and Henry S. Dawson proprietors and owners of the Town of Pine Bluff in the County of Jefferson and State of Arkansas of the first part and Joseph Rosati, Bishop of St. Louis of the other part. Witnesseth that the said parties of the first part for the purpose of promoting the erection of a Catholic Church in the Town of Pine Bluff aforesaid and for the consideration of the sum of five dollars to them in hand paid by the said party of the second part-----the receipt of which is hereby acknowledged they the said parties of the first part have this day and do by these present grant, bargain, sell, and release unto said Joseph Rosati, Bishop of aforesaid in trust to him and his successors for the use of the Catholic Church for ever all that tract or parcel of land situated, lying and being in the said Town of Pine Bluff, County and State aforesaid and known in the Plat of the same as lot number four (No. 4) of Block number Thirteen (No. 13) to have and to hold the same for the purpose herein specified unto him the said Joseph Rosati and his successors forever and the said parties of the first part for themselves, their heirs.-----------------etc.

In testimony where of we have said parties of the frist part do hereunto set their hands and affix their seals this day and year above written.

                                        A. H. Davis   (Seal)
                                        Jas. J. Chowning (Seal)
                                        Wm M. Pinckard   (Seal)
                                        Henry S. Dawson   (Seal)

Deed to property at Pullen and Georgia Streets, Pine Bluff—7 July 1838.

was sent by the first Bishop of Little Rock, Bishop Andrew Byrne. Father Clarke also made visits to surrounding missions during his pastorate between 1858 and 1864. We conclude that a small church existed in Pine Bluff many years before 1858.[4]

The Reverend Francis Laughran served during the year 1867 and later that year, the Reverend Phillip Shannahan from 1867 to 1868. The first administration of the Sacrament of Confirmation was on 8 December 1867, by The Most Reverend Edward Fitzgerald, D.D. the second Bishop of Little Rock. Those confirmed were: Frederick Scull, Edward Flood, Anne Hamilton, Florence Beomis, Eleanora Carroll, Felicia Carroll, Manette Mary Hamilton, and Mary Crubin.[5]

Chapter 8
St. Joseph's Church, West Sixth Avenue

In the year 1869, the Catholic Parish in Pine Bluff received a donation of land from Mr. William B. Scull and his wife Cordelia Rabron Scull. This land fronting 80 feet on Broadway (now West Sixth Avenue) and running south 416 feet. At this time this piece of land was on the edge of town. No streets

St. Joseph's Catholic Church, circa 1871. Note Rectory in background. Reproduction photography by Bryant.

St. Joseph's Catholic Church, circa 1888, showing apse added to church, and with the Rectory in the background. Photograph— "Pictorial History of Arkansas"—Hemstead.

Pew Rent receipt—1902. Courtesy of Mr. John Webkes.

ran southward, as all of the land to the south was still a forest.

The Reverend John B. Duggan was the pastor from 1868 to 1871. In 1871, the building committee, D. W. Carroll, J. Hewes Scull, and J. P. Murphy, let a contract for a small church to cost $3,000. Bell and Bocage were the contractors, with M. G. Morris, foreman. There was not enough money to complete the building, but it was put in a fair condition, and no debt was incurred.[1] A bazaar was held, the proceeds to help build a house for the pastor, to put up fences, and to make other improvements. Mrs. L. P. Scull was president of this project, with Mrs. B. A. Holcombe as vice-

Pastor's Memorial Window in old St. Joseph's Church. Reproduction photography by Bryant.

president. The sum of $1,200 was realized from the Bazaar.[2]

In December of 1872, Bishop Fitzgerald sent the Reverend John M. Lucey to Pine Bluff. His labors in the parish, so untiringly given for forty-two years, are recorded elsewhere in this volume.

After his arrival in Pine Bluff, Father Lucey spent his time gathering up the scattered Catholics in this vicinity. He also labored as missionary in all of the southeastern part of Arkansas. In 1888 Father Lucey added a large apse to the church which had been built in 1871. This work and the renovation of the old church, cost the congregation about $10,000.[3]

In the East nave of Old St. Joseph's Church was located the Pastor's Memorial Window listing pastors of St. Mary's on one window, and the pastors of St. Joseph's on the other.[4]

In 1888 Father Lucey dedicated a window in the church to the memory of Saracen, last chief of the Quapaw Indians. This window was located to the right of the front entry on the side wall of the church (West side).[5] All of the stained glass windows were removed and stored when the old church gave

Original Saracen Window in old St. Joseph's Church. Reproduction photography by Bryant.

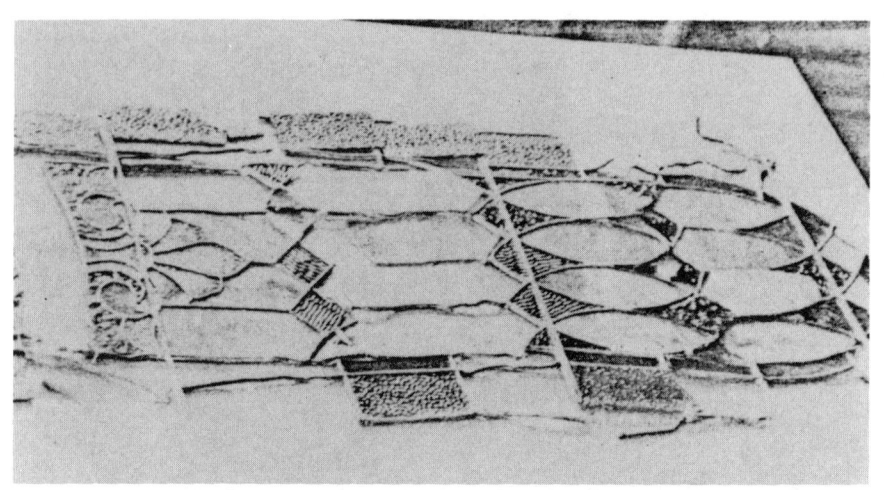

"Saracen Window" as it looked when found. Photograph, courtesy, The Guardian, *Little Rock, Ark.*, 13 Nov. 1970.

Composite window in the Jefferson County Public Library.

Annunciation Academy building with St. Anthony's Chapel under arrow to left and rear. Reproduction photography by Bryant.

way to the present St. Joseph's Church building. From that time on, there is no real knowledge of the actual Saracen window. For months, several years ago, conscientious historians and artisans, with the permission of Bishop Fletcher, had worked diligently to locate what was believed to be the famous "Saracen Window," and to restore it.[6]

This window now on display in the library of the Pine Bluff Civic Center, is a composite of two broken stained glass windows found in a dusty niche beneath St. Peter's Church in Pine Bluff.[7]

In 1880, Father Lucey had succeeded in inducing the Sisters of Charity of Nazareth to come to Pine Bluff and begin their Academy.[8] Of this Academy, the reader is referred to the chapter covering this institution, which appears elsewhere in this writing.

In 1907, Monsignor Lucey published a handbook and presented it to the Catholics of Pine Bluff: "wherein to find the necessary information concerning St. Joseph's Church." The names and addresses of Catholic families of St. Joseph's was given as of December 1907.[9]

By 1911, the annual report of the Pastor showed several interesting facts concerning the "Societies" of St. Joseph's Church. There were then about 125 families.[10]

Directly behind old St. Joseph's Church was St. Anthony's Chapel. The entrance faced the Academy building to the West. This chapel was dismantled sometime before the old church building was moved in about 1913.

Handbook, 1907.

Marx-Baer Grocery Co.

———— Headquarters for ————

———— SOMETHING GOOD TO EAT ————

AGENTS
Chase and Sanborn's Coffees and Teas
Berg's Kosher Sausage
Ferndell Line Pure Food Products

Both Phones

Daroux, B. J., 921 East Second avenue.
Daroux, Ernest, 921 East Second avenue.
Daroux, Arthur, 921 East Second avenue.
Daroux, Mrs. Harriett, 921 East Second avenue.
Daroux, George, 919 East Second avenue.
Daley, H. H., 816 Main street.
Daley, Mrs. Carolina, 816 Main street.
Davis, Mrs. Victoria, 207 Missouri street.
DePrima, Michael, 406 Main street.
DePrima, Mrs. Frances, 406 Main street.
Dellmon, Charles, 701 State street.
Dellmon, Mrs. Hazel, 701 State street.
Dellmon, Miss Ethel, 701 State street.
Dellmon, Miss Bertha, 701 State street.
Dellmon, J. H., 721 Texas street.
Dellmon, Mrs. Mary, 721 Texas street.
Dempsey, Mrs. Mary, 618 Morris street.
Dempsey, Miss Clara, 618 Morris street.
Dempsey, Robert, 618 Morris street.
Depatie, Fred, 617 West Fourth avenue.

Derrisseux, Mrs. Mary, 216 East Second avenue.
Dolan, John, 600 East Third avenue.
Donovan, John, 118 Louisiana street.
Donovan, Mrs. Mary, 118 Louisiana street.
Donovan, Mae, 213 West Barraque street.
Donovan, Matt, 627 East Second avenue.
Donovan, Mrs. Alcen, 627 East Second avenue.
Doran, Ed, Gardener's House, East Third avenue.
Doran, John, Gardener's House, East Third avenue.
Dowd, Miss Nellie, 709 East Sixth avenue.
Dowd, James, 709 East Sixth avenue.
Dowling, David, 419 East Sixth avenue.
Drake, James, 400 West Barraque street.
Durner, Mrs. Mary, 617 East Second avenue.
Durrin, Henry, 701 State street.
Dwyer, W. T., 500 East Twelfth avenue.
Ellis, Sidney, 621 East Second avenue.
Ellis, Mrs. Mary, 621 East Second avenue.
Elsner, Theresa, 1115 West Fourth avenue.
Emmett, C. F., Warren Road.
Emmett, Miss Bobbie, Warren Road.
Emmett, Patrick, Warren Road.
Emmett, Clifton, Warren Road.
Enderby, Mrs. Ethel, 1113 East Third avenue.
Enderby, Fred, 1113 East Third avenue.
English, E., 617 East Second avenue.
Evans, W. H., 814 West Fourteenth avenue.
Evans, Mrs. Elizabeth, 814 West Fourteenth avenue.
Feeley, Charles, 600 East Sixth avenue.
Ferguson, Will, 1208 East Second avenue.
Ferguson, Mrs. Edna, 1206 East Second avenue.
Ferguson, Miss Eliza, 1113 East Third avenue.
Ferguson, Miss Regina, 1113 East Third avenue.
Ferguson, Miss Veronica, 1113 East Third avenue.
Fessler, Mrs. Sophia, 2916 Scull street.
Fallin, Edward, 1319 East Second avenue.
Fallin, Mrs. Mary, 1319 East Second avenue.
Foster, Martin, 603 East Third avenue.
Foti, F., 812 Main street.
Foti, Mrs. Rosana, Third avenue and State street.
Foti, Jakey, Third avenue and State street.
Foti, John, Third avenue and State street.

—50—

BUCK'S STOVES AND RANGES

And a Complete Line of

Furniture and House Furnishings

Prices Reasonable—Cash or Credit

Reap-Crawford Furniture Co.

307 W. Second Avenue.   PINE BLUFF, ARK.

Foti, Mrs. Rosa, Third avenue and State street.
Foti, Frank, Third avenue and State street.
Foti, Mrs. Mary, Third avenue and State street.
Foti, Frank P., Third avenue and State street.
Foti, Joseph, Third avenue and State street.
Fox, J. C., 1302 West Fifth avenue.
Fox, Miss Birdie, 1302 West Sixth avenue.
Fox, Miss Mary, 1302 West Sixth avenue.
Francis, P. J., 709 East Sixth avenue.
Franey, Mrs. Mary, 709 East Sixth avenue.
Franey, Mrs. Catherine, 1168 Tennessee street.
Franey, Miss Anastasia, 1168 Tennessee street.
Franey, Frank, 1168 Tennessee street.
Franey, Anthony, 1168 Tennessee street.
Franey, Miss Catherine, 1168 Tennessee street.
Franey, William, 627 East Second avenue.
Frazier, L., 1017 Indiana street.
Frentel, Miss Josie, 1027 East Second avenue.
Gallagher, Mrs. Mary, 709 East Second avenue.
Gallagher, Dr. H. H., 918 West Fifth avenue.
Gallagher, Met, 918 West Fifth avenue.
Gang, Peter, 1900 Georgia street.
Gang, Mrs. Frances, 1900 Georgia street.
Gang, Frank, 1900 Georgia street.
Garney, Mrs. Hannah, 1618 East Fourth avenue.
Garney, Charles, 1618 East Fourth avenue.
Garney, Anthony, 1618 East Fourth avenue.

Garney, George, 1618 East Fourth avenue.
Garrison, Mrs. Ada, 717 East Second avenue.
Gaske, W., 1913 East Second avenue.
Gaske, Mrs. Victoria, 1913 East Second avenue.
Gaske, Miss Mary, 1913 East Second avenue.
Gaske, Miss Anna, 1913 East Second avenue.
Gaske, Felix, 1913 East Second avenue.
Genevay, Mrs. K., 603 East Third avenue.
Genevay, Felix, 603 East Third avenue.
Gill, Miss Lizzie, 107 East Second avenue.
Gockwin, Miss Angie, 711 East Third avenue.
Graham, Mrs. Mary, 1121 West Sixth avenue.
Griffin, James.
Haislip, Mrs. Millie, 1221 West Sixth avenue.
Hallans, Mrs., 618 Nebraska street.
Hajiul, Mrs., 2209 West Sixth avenue.
Hanson, Mrs. Angelina, East of Town.
Harkness, Lee, 704 East Second avenue.
Harkness, Mrs. Clara, 704 East Second avenue.
Harkness, Raymond, 704 East Second avenue.
Hart, Harvey, 209 Ohio street.
Hart, Mrs. Elizabeth, 209 Ohio street.
Harvey, E. B., 122 East Second avenue.
Harvey, Mrs. Amanda, 122 East Second avenue.
Harvey, James, 122 East Second avenue.
Heisoing, John, 2012 Colorado street.
Heissoing, Mrs. Mary, 2012 Colorado street.
Helm, Mrs. Ellen, 415 East Second avenue.
Hemsteger, Mrs. Mary, 218 West Fifth avenue.
Hendricks, Mrs. M., 204 East Barraque street.
Hill, Mrs. Anna, 600 East Barraque street.
Hoffman, Mrs. Eliza, 108 East Ninth avenue.
Holcombe, Mrs. B. A., 829 West Fifth avenue.
Holland, John, 802 West Barraque street.
Holland, Mrs. Minnie, 802 West Barraque street.
Holland, Albert, 802 West Barraque street.
Holland, Michael, 216 East Second avenue.
Holland, Mrs. Anna, 600 East Sixth avenue.
Hooper, George, 1901 East Barraque street.
Hope, Mrs. DeWitt, 619 Tennessee street.
Hopkins, Mrs. Mary, 20 East Poplar street.
Hosler, Mrs. Jane, 617 East Second avenue.

—51—

Howard, H., 701 Mulberry street.
Hoyler, Mrs. Fred, 1419 Main street.
Huber, Mrs. Mary, 1928 East Second avenue.
Huggard, Mrs. Emma, 816 Texas street.
Huggard, Thomas, 600 East Third avenue.
Ish, Mrs. Annie, 829 East Third avenue.
Ivy, Mrs. Annie, 509 West Sixth avenue.
Jabbur, Eliah, 611 East Sixth avenue.
Jackson, ———, 709 State street.
Jacob, Joe, 611 East Sixth avenue.
James, John, Dreyfus' store.
Jenkins, Dr. J. L. 319 West Fourth avenue.
Johnson, Henry, 719 East Third avenue.
Johnson, Mrs. Matilda, 719 East Third avenue.
Johnson, Miss Lily, 719 East Third avenue.
Johnson, Frank, 719 East Third avenue.
Johnson, Miss Ruth, 719 East Third avenue.
Johnson, Mrs. Elizabeth, 819 West Fourteenth avenue.
Johnson, Mrs. Josephine, 1113 East Third avenue.
Jones, Mrs. Anna, 218 West Second avenue.
Jones, Edward, 1611 East Fifth avenue.
Keeley, Will, 723 Walnut street.
Keeley, Miss Mary, 723 Walnut street.
Kennedy, John, 921 East Second avenue.
Kennedy, Mrs. John, 921 East Second avenue.
Kerwin, Mrs. Ellen, 600 East Third avenue.
Kerwin, Mrs. Mrg., 600 East Third avenue.
Kerwin, E. J., 600 East Third avenue.
Kerwin, Mrs. Carolina, 600 East Third avenue.
Kerwin, John, 600 East Third avenue.
King, F. P., 511 Oak street.
King, Mrs. F. P., 511 Oak street.
Kohlbrenner, Mrs. Mary, 1818 East Barraque street.
Kohlbrenner, Henry, 1818 East Barraque street.
Kohlbrenner, Miss Rose, 1818 East Barraque street.
Kohlbrenner, Louis, 1818 East Barraque street.
Koster, L, Seventh avenue and Ohio street.
Koury, Joe, 611 East Sixth avenue.
Kuhner, Felix, 1000 East Second avenue.
Kuhner, Mary, 1000 East Second avenue.
Lamonica, Mrs. Mary, 220 East Second avenue.
Lamonica, Miss Rose, 220 East Second avenue.

Lamonica, Ada, 220 East Second avenue.
Lamonica, Miss Fannie, 220 East Second avenue.
Lamonica, Bernard, 220 East Second avenue.
Lamonica, Lee, 220 East Second avenue.
Lampert, Bern, 1307 East Third avenue.
Lampert, Fred, 1305 East Third avenue.
Lampert, Mrs. Louise, 1305 East Third avenue.
Lampert, Mrs. Catherine, 213 East Second avenue.
Laxton, Mrs. Jennie, 803 West Fourth avenue.
Lazzarani, Natahna, 715 Texas street.
Lehman, A, 809 East Third avenue.
Lehman, Mrs. Mary, 809 East Third avenue.
Lehman, Miss Josephine, 809 East Third avenue.
Lehnert, Mrs. Gussie, 420 West Eighth avenue.
Lehnert, Miss Annie, 420 West Eighth avenue.
Lehnert, John, 420 West Eighth avenue.
Lewis, Mrs. Charles, 800 West Fifteenth avenue.
Liberty, D., 621 East Second avenue.
Limbaugh, Jas. 709 Main street.
List, Miss Amalie, 612 Beech street.
Locardi, Jos., 215 East Third avenue.
Locardi, Mrs. Theresa, 215 East Third avenue.
Locardi, Peter, 215 East Third avenue.
Locardi, John, 215 East Third avenue.
Locardi, Victor, 215 East Third avenue.
Locardi, Pio, 215 East Third avenue.
Lovejoy, Mrs. George, 812 East Second avenue.
Lovelady, Mrs. Mary, 621 Tennessee street.
Luperini, Angelo, 326 Main street.
Lynch, Mrs. Catherine, Twenty-first and Marble.
McCarthy, C. F., 1617 West Ninth avenue.
McCarthy, Mrs. Catherine, 1617 West Ninth avenue.
McCoy, Jim, 707 East Second avenue.
McGaughey, Joseph, 707 East Third avenue.
McGaughey, Mrs. Stella, 814 Walnut street.
McGinn, 1011 East Tenth avenue.
McKnight, James, 1510 East Sixth avenue.
McKnight, Thomas, 1510 East Sixth avenue.
McKnight, John, 1510 East Sixth avenue.
McNulty, A., 2300 West Sixteenth avenue.
McNulty, Mrs. Salina, 2300 West Sixteenth avenue.
McTierney, Peter, 1912 East Fourth avenue.

McTierney, Miss Nellie, 1912 East Fourth avenue.
Mahar, Mrs. Johannah, 701 East Third avenue.
Maiani, Adams, 412 West Sixth avenue.
Mahoney, John, 316 West Fifth avenue.
Manzer, Mrs., 311 Olive street.
Mara, Mrs. M. L., 316 West Fifth avenue.
Mara, Will, 316 West Fifth avenue.
Marino, Neildo, 406 Main street.
Marshall, J. L., 1429 Ohio street.
Mattmiller, Mrs. Lulu, 705 Texas street.
Matz, John, 1027 East Second avenue.
Matz, Mrs. Rosa, 1027 East Second avenue.
Matz, Charles, 1027 East Second avenue.
Matz, Miss Stella, 1027 East Second avenue.
Matz, Nick, 2010 East Seventh avenue.
Matz, Mrs. Elizabeth, 2010 East Seventh avenue.
Mayer, Mrs. Amalia, 816 East Second avenue.
Mayer, Miss Ida, 816 East Second avenue.
Mayer, Joseph, 816 East Second avenue.
Merlo, Pio, East of Town.
Merlo, Mrs. Mary, East of Town.
Merlo, John, East of Town.
Merlo, James, East of Town.
Merlo, Miss Mary, East of Town.
Merrick, Mrs., 2006 East Barraque street.
Merrill, Joe, 1115 East Third avenue.
Merrill, Mrs. Albina, 1115 East Barraque street.
Mayer, Mrs. Rosa, 1005 West Second avenue.
Mayer, Miss Lily, 1005 West Second avenue.
Mayer, Charles, 1005 West Second avenue.
Michael, Mrs. Mary, 611 East Sixth avenue.
Michael, Eliah, 611 East Sixth avenue.
Michelotti, Eugene, 326 Main street.
Michelotti, Joseph, 326 Main street.
Michelotti, Gabriel, 715 Texas street.
Michelotti, Mrs. Naterlina, 715 Texas street.
Michelotti, Pierre, 715 Texas street.
Miller, Mrs. Albertina, 618 East Second avenue.
Miller, William, 618 East Second avenue.
Miller, Nathaniel, 920 West Second avenue.
Miller, Mrs. Theresa, 920 West Second avenue.
Monestra, Toney, 406 Main street.

Monestra, Samuel, 406 Main street.
Montaique, Miss Augusta, 323 West Sixth avenue.
Montaique, C. H., 1204 East Sixth avenue.
Mooney, H. A., 820 Walnut street.
Mooney, Mrs. Mary, 820 Walnut street.
Mooney, Augustine, 820 Walnut street.
Mooney, Joseph, 820 Walnut street.
Mooney, Thomas, 820 Walnut street.
Mooney, William, 820 Walnut street.
Moore, C. F., 702 West Second avenue.
Moore, Mrs. C. F., 702 West Second avenue.
Moreau, Robert, 510 East Second avenue.
Morris, M. J. 1304 West Fourteenth avenue.
Morrow, G. W., 418 East Fifth avenue.
Morrow, Mrs. A., 418 East Fifth avenue.
Moser, Joseph, 1111 East Fifth avenue.
Moser, Mrs. Theresa, 1111 East Fifth avenue.
Moser, Miss Lena, 1111 East Fifth avenue.
Moser, Miss Lizzie, 1111 East Fifth avenue.
Moser, Miss Jennie, 1111 East Fifth avenue.
Moser, Miss Nellie, 1111 East Fifth avenue.
Moser, Oswald, 1111 East Fifth avenue.
Mountain, Miss Grace, 422 West Sixth avenue.
Mountain, Miss Mary, 600 East Fifth avenue.
Murphy, Carter, 809 West Second avenue.
Murphy, Mrs. Barbara, 809 West Second avenue.
Mustacchia, Nick, 803 West Ninth avenue.
Mustacchia, Mrs. Mary, 803 West Ninth avenue.
Mustacchia, Antonio, 803 West Ninth avenue.
Mustacchia, Peter, 803 West Ninth avenue.
Mustacchia, Mrs. Pearl, 803 West Ninth avenue.
Mustacchia, Joseph, 803 West Ninth avenue.
Mustacchia, John, 803 West Ninth avenue.
Mustacchia, Mrs. Anna, 803 West Ninth avenue.
Mustacchia, Frank, 803 West Ninth avenue.
Mustacchia, Paschal, 520 Louisiana street.
Mustacchia, Mrs. Luisi, 520 Louisiana street.
Myers, D. J., 1221 Cherry street.
Norris, Mrs. A. M., 218 West Second avenue.
Oaks, Mrs. Nellie, 620 Cherry street.
O'Brien, Mrs. J., 211 Louisiana street.
O'Connell, John, 323 West Sixth avenue.

O'Connell, Mrs. Emma, 323 West Sixth avenue.
O'Connell, Miss Lena, 323 West Sixth avenue.
O'Connell, Miss Leicester, 323 West Sixth avenue.
O'Keiff, Jack, 414 West Barraque street
O'Keiff, Mrs. Scottie, 414 West Barraque street.
O'Keiff, Mrs. Elizabeth, 64 South Linden street.
O'Neil, Mrs. Louisa, 1007 East Second avenue
O'Neil, Mrs. Nellie, 1007 East Second avenue
O'Neil, Charlie, 1007 East Second avenue.
O'Neil, Miss Irene, 1007 East Second avenue.
O'Neil, John, 702 East Second avenue.
O'Neil, Martin, 702 East Second avenue.
Ormsie, Jos., 1304 East Sixth avenue.
Ormsie, Mrs. Josephine, 1304 East Sixth avenue.
Paechtel, Miss Lena, 930 West Second avenue.
Paechtel, Miss Catherine, 930 West Second avenue.
Parker, Francis, 105 Pennsylvania street.
Parker, Mrs. Mary, 105 Pennsylvania street.
Parker, Joseph, 105 Pennsylvania street.
Parker, Charles, 105 Pennsylvania street.
Patterson, Mrs. Emily, 508 East Sixth avenue.
Paull, Mrs. A., 502 West Second avenue
Payne, Mrs. Caroline, 705 Texas avenue.
Peterson, Mrs. A., 8 South Tennessee street.
Phelps, Mrs. Mary, 701 East Third avenue.
Phelps, Miss Sadie, 707 East Third avenue
Phelps, Miss Mary, 707 East Third avenue.
Picchi, Peter, 810 East Sixth avenue.
Picchi, Miss Elizabeth, 810 East Sixth avenue.
Picket, Mrs. Agnes, 701 East Third avenue.
Picket, Miss Ruth, 701 East Third avenue.
Pinkney, Pembroke, 718 West Sixth avenue.
Pinkney, Mrs. Anna, 718 West Sixth avenue.
Parlis, Mrs. Mary, 216 East Second avenue.
Powers, Mrs., Third Avenue Hotel.
Rebeccah, Gasparo, 820 West Second avenue.
Rebeccah, Mrs. Josephine, 820 West Second avenue.
Rebeccah, Miss Mary, 820 West Second avenue.
Rebeccah, Miss Carinne, 820 West Second avenue.
Rebeccah, George, 820 West Second avenue.
Rebeccah, Myhause, 820 West Second avenue.
Redding, Ed. 614 Texas street.

Remond, Mrs. Mary, 820 Walnut street.
Reynolds, Mrs. Carolina, Nineteenth and Pine.
Reynolds, Henry, Nineteenth and Pine.
Reynolds, Miss Ellen, Nineteenth and Pine.
Price, Mrs. Benj., 816 West Fifteenth avenue.
Reder, Fred, 1133 East Second avenue.
Riley, Mrs., 315 East Fifth avenue.
Roberts, Mrs., 519 Georgia street.
Russell, 219 West Fifth avenue.
Rottet, R. B., 803 East Second avenue.
Rottet, Mrs. Lillian, 803 East Second avenue.
Royston, Francis, 707 West Sixth avenue.
Schlemer, John, 868 East Second avenue
Schlemer, Mrs. Carolina, 868 East Second avenue
Schlemer, John, 868 East Second.
Schrader, Ernest, 1202 East Fifth avenue.
Schrader, Mrs. Anme, 1202 East Fifth avenue.
Scott, Miss, 310 Olive street.
Seull, Ben, 310 Ash street.
Seull, Miss Blanche, 310 Ash street.
Seull, Mrs. Ed, 310 Ash street.
Seull, Knox, 320 West Barraque.
Seull, Mrs. Sadie, 320 West Barraque street.
Seull, Mrs. L. P., 320 West Barraque avenue.
Sennett, Mrs. Beulah, 1021 West Second avenue.
Seymore, Mrs. Belle, 818 Cherry street.
Seymore, Asa F., 818 Cherry street.
Sherman, Joe, 502 West Barraque street.
Sherry, Mrs. Mary, 1210 East Third avenue.
Sherry, Charles, 1210 East Third avenue.
Sherry, George, 1210 East Third avenue.
Shinall, Mrs. C. P., 2107 East Barraque street.
Shares, Mrs. Agnes, 809 East Second avenue.
Simmons, W. M., 1060 Ohio street.
Smith, Mrs. 719 East Second avenue.
Smith, Dr. C. D., 1203 West Sixth avenue.
Smith, Mrs. Gertrude, 1200 West Sixth avenue.
Smith, Miss Mary, 1200 West Sixth avenue.
Smith, Julius, 600 East Sixth avenue.
Smith, Mrs. Mary, 600 East Sixth avenue.
Smith, Arthur, 600 East Sixth avenue
Smith, Clarence, 600 East Sixth avenue.

Soloman, A. John, 611 East Sixth avenue.
Soloman, Abraham, 611 East Sixth avenue.
Soloman, Elias, 611 East Sixth avenue.
Steele, Mrs. Mary, Twentieth and Poplar.
Steele, Miss Mary, Twentieth and Poplar.
Steele, John, Twentieth and Poplar.
Stovecan, Ernest, 1006 West Fourth avenue.
Strobel, Frank, 1702 East Fourth avenue.
Strobel, E., 1212 West Fifth avenue.
Sullivan, Robert, 313 West Second avenue.
Sullivan, Mrs. Ida, 313 West Second avenue.
Sylvester, Ben, 1116 West Fourth avenue.
Sylvester, Mrs. Anna, 1116 West Fourth avenue.
Sylvester, Charles, Fourth avenue and Cherry street.
Sylvester, Mrs. Philomena, Fourth and Cherry.
Taggart, M. O., 603 West Second avenue.
Taggart, Mrs. Marian, 603 West Second avenue.
Taggart, Miss Alymer, 603 West Second avenue.
Taggart, Goy, 603 West Second avenue.
Tague, J., 210 East Eighth avenue.
Tague, Paul, 210 East Eighth avenue.
Tague, Miss Mary, 210 East Eighth avenue.
Tayler, Miss Jettie, 705 Texas street.
Terry, Mrs. H. C., 2001 East Pullen street.
Terry, Francis, 2001 East Pullen street.
Terry, Charlie, 2001 East Pullen street.
Tierney, Patrick, 1210 East Twentieth avenue.
Thompson, Mrs. Agnes, 1909 Cherry street.
Tamaszewski, Mrs. Frances, 610 Texas street.
Tamaszewski, Caesar, 610 Texas street.
Tamaszewski, John, 610 Texas street.
Tamaszewski, Miss Blanche, 610 Texas street.
Tschann, Miss Lidie, 412 West Sixth avenue.
Vaughn, Mrs. A. P., 1010 Plum street.
Vaughn, Miss Frances, 1010 Plum street.
Verret, E. 1920 West Pullen street.
Verret, Mrs. Lema, 1920 Pullen street.
Vourel, Miss Lena, 101 East Third avenue.
Waddell, C. P., 705 East Second avenue.
Walker, Miss Virginia, 1021 West Second avenue.
Walker, Miss Eulabe, 1021 West Second avenue.
Walker, Miss Beulah, 1021 West Second avenue.

Waskoski, Jos., 1816 East Pullen street.
Waskoski Mrs. Catherine, 1816 East Pullen street
Waskoski, Frederick, 1816 East Pullen street.
Waskoski, Jun, 1820 East Pullen street.
Waskoski, Mrs. J., 1820 East Pullen street.
Weaver, Mrs. Anna, 1202 Cherry street.
Weaver, Milford, 215 West Fifteenth avenue.
Weaver, Mrs. Catherine, 215 West Fifteenth avenue.
Weaver, Ernest, 215 West Fifteenth avenue.
Weaver, Miss Thel, 215 West Fifteenth avenue.
Weaver, Millard J., 215 West Fifteenth avenue.
Webkes, Henry, 804 East Second avenue.
Webkes, Mrs. Golden, 804 East Second avenue.
Welch, R., 34 West Second avenue.
Werling, Francis, 405 East Sixth avenue.
Werling, Mrs. Elizabeth, 405 East Sixth avenue.
Werling, Miss Anna, 405 East Sixth avenue.
Werling, Oscar, 405 East Sixth avenue.
Werling, Frank, 44 East Sixth avenue.
Werling, Mrs. Nellie, 44 East Sixth avenue.
Werling, Roy, 44 East Sixth avenue.
Werling, Frank, 44 East Sixth avenue.
White, Mrs. Emma, 422 West Eighth avenue.
White, Allan, 422 West Eighth avenue.
Wilkins, Mrs. Mollie 1014 West Fifth avenue.
Williams, Joe, 611 East Sixth avenue.
Williams, Ramon, 611 East Sixth avenue.
Williams, B., 800 East Sixth avenue.
Williams, Mrs. B., 800 East Sixth avenue.
Williams, Warren, 704 East Sixth avenue.
Williams, Mrs. Etta, 704 East Sixth avenue.
Withers, Mrs. Julia, 1223 West Sixth avenue.
Withers, Miss Josephine, 1223 West Sixth avenue.
Wise, Mrs. Mary, 2100 East Barraque street.
Wolff, Mrs. B. C., 82 West Pullen street.
Woods, J., 312 Olive street.
Wright, Charles, 402 West Seventh avenue.
Wright, Mrs. Stella, 402 West Seventh avenue.
Wright, Mrs. A. M., 714 Olive street.
Wright, Miss Winifrid, 714 Olive street.
Winifrid, 714 Olive street.

SOCIETIES OF ST. JOSEPH'S CHURCH.

Ladies' Altar Society.

MRS. J. B. WHITE, President.
J. T. DAVIS, Secretary.

Membership of 1911, 65.

Balance from 1910	$ 21.63
Receipts of Year 1911	184.15
Expenditures of Year 1911	175.13
Balance in Treasury, Dec. 31, 1911	$30.65

St. Joseph's Cemetery—Sale of Lots, Fencing, Etc.
In charge of Pastor.

Excess of Expenditures of 1910	$ 11.61
Expenditures of 1911	105.35
	$116.96
Receipts from sale of Lots	32.00
Excess of Expenditures	$84.96

St. Joseph's Cemetery Association.

W. O. TAGGART, President.
MRS. W. A. BISHOP, Secretary.

Membership of 1911, 68.

Expenditures of Association 1911, To Sexton	$ 109.75
Receipts of Association 1911	107.25
Excess of Expenditures	$2.50

Knights of Columbus.

Number of Membership 1911, 101.

Jules T. Borresen, Grand Knight.   John Kirchgraber, Fin. Secy.

League of the Sacred Heart.
Membership, 200.

Rt. Rev. J. M. Lucy, V. G. Director.   Miss Virginia Walker, Secy.

Sodality of Holy Angiers—Membership of 1911, 41. **Miss Mary Holland, President; M. H. Taggart, Vice-President.**
Sodality of Sacred Heart—Membership of 1911, 30. Leo Harkness, President; Miss Kate Boyce, Vice-President.
St. Joseph's Sunday School—Enrollment of 1911, **124.**
(Sisters of Charity Teachers).
Annunciation Academy—Conducted by **Sisters of Charity of** Nazareth. Annual enrollment, 218.

Annual Report, 1911.

FOR YEAR ENDING DECEMBER 31, 1911.

GENERAL SUMMARY.

General receipts, 1911	$2,095.25
Subscriptions for support of Church or pew rent	1,235.50
Sunday plate collections	655.75
Altar Society receipts	184.15
Cemetery Association dues	107.25
Men's subscription to buy diamond ring for bazaar	100.00
Grand Total	$4,377.90

SPIRITUAL AFFAIRS.

Number of Baptisms in 1911	24
Number of Marriages in 1911	10
Interments in St. Joseph's Cemetery, Including 2 Colored	15
Number of Holy Communions	5,183

Number of Families.—There are about 125 families in St. Joseph's Parish, made up of Bohemians, French, English, German, Italian, Irish, Spanish and American. The receipts are over $300.00 short of the usual amount this year, owing chiefly to the absence of the Pastor at Little Rock the first six months of the year, and to the fact that there has been no regular assistant Priest

Respectfully submitted,

J. M. LUCEY, V. G. Pastor.

I have examined the books of St. Joseph's Church and find the account well kept and correct.

T. M. DOYLE, Accountant.

The above report of Rt. Rev. J. M. Lucey, V. G. Pastor of St. Joseph's Church is hereby approved.

JOHN H. DELLMON,

MIKE HOLLAND,

JOHN J. KERWIN,

W. O. TAGGART,

R. L. HARKNESS,

BEN SYLVESTER.

Wardens of St. Joseph's Church.

Pine Bluff, Ark., Jan. 1st, 1912.

Monsignor Lucey had for a long time cherished a fond dream of seeing a splendid new church erected in Pine Bluff. At that time, it was estimated that such a church could be built for $50,000. The Bishop of Little Rock contributed $5,000 towards this worthy project. In 1913, Monsignor Lucey had the old church moved about one hundred feet east, and the priest's house moved further back. He began the erection of the new church; the foundation was begun and completed. Monsignor Lucey wished to continue the good work, but his health had been failing for some time.[12]

Monsignor Lucey's death occured in June of 1914, and in September of 1914, Bishop Morris, third Bishop of Little Rock, sent the Reverend Patrick Enright to replace him. On 10 January 1915, Father Enright was elevated to Right Reverend Monsignor. Monsignor Enright had the priest's house renovated and veneered.[13] Just two years later, Monsignor Enright died, on 10 April 1917.

Monsignor Enright's successor was the Reverend Patrick J. Higgins, who spent five years as pastor at Pine Bluff. He worked hard to augment the new church fund. When Father Higgins resigned his pastorate in April 1922 because of poor health, the new church fund had nearly $40,000.[14]

Chapter 9

St. Joseph's Church, 1922 to the Present Time

In April of 1922, the Reverend Walter J. Tynin was sent to Pine Bluff. Father Tynin's first thought on coming to Pine Bluff was to build the new church. The plans and specifications had been drawn by Mr. Edward T. P. Graham, a celebrated architect of Boston, Massachusetts. (These plans were slightly altered.)[1] The foundation erected by Monsignor Lucey was thus fully utilized, and the contract was let 21 April 1922.[2] A few months later, the contractor died, and they (the building committee) were fortunate in securing the services of Mr. M. M. Bruce, a convert to the Catholic faith. Mr. Bruce began his work by strengthening the foundations and piers for the columns in the church.[3]

The church is a structure of Roman Basilica style. It is built of Malvern matt faced brick and trimmed with stone. The columns are of Indiana white orletic stone. The church is 143 feet long, by 67 feet wide. It will comfortably seat 610 people, but 800 can easily be accommodated.[4]

The main altar, imported from Italy is cut from Carrara marble and assembled in the Byzantine style. It is a large altar, the table being 10 feet in length. The Tabernacle is of gold and of graceful design. Above the Tabernacle is a large and impressive Crucifixion group. The Relic enclosed in the Altar stone is said to be of Saint Beatrice.[5] This main Altar is flanked on each side by large stone figures of angels holding Sanctuary lamps which are burned alternately.[6]

The side Altars for St. Joseph and for the Blessed Virgin are duplicates of the main altar, and also are Carrara marble. A marble Communion rail of symmetrical beauty was installed, as well as the beautiful Stations of the

Architect's drawing for St. Joseph's Church, circa 1921. Photograph, courtesy of Mr. Tim Massanelli.

Present view of St. Joseph's Catholic Church.

Main Altar and Altar of Sacrifice, St. Joseph's Church.

Cross, carved from stone in bas-relief, tinted in pastel shades, and set into niches in the east and west walls.[7]

The corner stone for the new church was laid by His Excellency, John B. Morris, D.D., Bishop of Little Rock, on Sunday, 18 June 1922. The church was dedicated by Bishop Morris with the solemn ceremonial of the Catholic Church on Sunday, 14 October 1923. The music on this grand occassion was rendered by the choir of St. John's Diocesan Seminary of Little Rock.[8]

During his pastorate in Pine Bluff, Father Tynin was made Dean of Southeastern Arkansas by Bishop Morris. In October of 1930, Father Tynin was transferred to Holy Redeemer Church, El Dorado, Arkansas, and then in November of 1930, Bishop Morris sent the Very Reverend Gregory H. Keller to Pine Bluff.[9]

Father Keller's labors in Pine Bluff at St. Joseph's Church were very fruitful. Care of the missions was broadened and the Holy Sacrifice of the

Procession at the laying of the cornerstone, St. Joseph's Church, 1922. Photograph, courtesy of Mr. John Webkes.

Mass was offered each Sunday in one of the three mission churches (St. Mary's, Plum Bayou; St. Patrick's, Sulphur Springs and Blessed Sacrament of Grady, Arkansas).[10]

Father Keller's administration as pastor was during the Great Depression years. A number of families had moved from the parish, and it was necessary to discontinue the high school department of Annunciation Academy. The church income was low, due to the general economic condition during this depression era. When St. Joseph's Church was built, the cost of building in 1923 was so much more than the funds available, that it was necessary for Father Tynin and the Wardens of St. Joseph's to negotiate a loan. This indebtedness had been extended into Father Keller's administration. The debt was reduced as much as possible with the lean funds available. This debt was not completely retired during Father Keller's tenure as Pastor.[11]

In 1937, the marble Holy Water fonts were moved from the side doors of the church, and placed at the front doors. Moderately priced hanging fonts were purchased for use at each side entrance.

In March of 1938, Father Keller read a report of the collections to the Board of Wardens, comparing the average weekly amount with the proceeding years, as follows:

1931—$105.29
1932—$ 91.79
1933—$ 94.71

1934—$ 96.80
1935—$100.92
1936—$102.22
1937—$106.04
1938—$110.63[12]

These sums were the total weekly average of contributions from the entire congregation. Keep in mind, our nation was then experiencing one of the greatest of economic depressions.

On 6 October 1940, Bishop Morris assigned the Reverend Thomas F. Walshe as pastor of St. Joseph's Church. Father Walshe was an aggressive and successful administrator, and many improvements were made during the time he was pastor at St. Joseph's.[13]

The Depression years were at last behind, and now our country was engaged in World War II. A large chemical arsenal was built at Pine Bluff, and many new families moved into this area of the state. The church income showed a marked increase, which enabled Monsignor Walshe to completely retire the church debt. He was also able to accumulate funds to make some much needed improvements.[14]

During his administration, Monsignor Walshe built the present brick rectory in 1941, at a cost of $10,634.11,[15] remodeled the old rectory into a Parish Hall, and in 1952 was responsible for the general repair and renovations to the church building.[16]

At this time (1952) accoustical tile was installed on the walls, which helped eliminate the cracking and falling plaster caused by a moisture condition. The pews were completely re-done and new floor tile was installed. A partition was erected inside the North entrance to the church, thereby creating a vestibule area, central heating was installed in the church, replacing two old wood burning stoves—all at a cost of more than $50,000.[17]

Stained glass windows were installed, to replace the old frosted glass windows (See Memorials). Monsignor Walshe solicited donors in the parish for the cost of these windows, and the parishioners generously contributed.[18]

The associate priests serving during these years were, Father N. Charles McGinnis, Father Charles F. Diamond (who left to join the service as Chaplain in the United States Army), Father Jesse Chaney, and Father William J. Burke.[19]

Monsignor Walshe was transferred to Fort Smith, Arkansas on 1 September 1954, and Bishop Fletcher assigned the Right Reverend Monsignor Joseph A. Gallagher to St. Joseph's Church. Monsignor Gallagher was Director of Vocations for 20 years, and during this time, through his close friendship and association with the late Cardinal Dennis Daugherty, Archbishop of Philadelphia, Monsignor Gallagher was instru-

East side view of Gallagher Hall.

mental in bringing to Arkansas, a large number of young men from Philadelphia, who would study for the priesthood at St. John's Seminary in Little Rock.[20]

In 1955 Monsignor Gallagher was responsible for having the church air conditioned at a cost of $15,000. There was no drive for funds, yet, voluntary contributions were made, and the balance of the cost was paid from the current church funds available at the time.

Monsignor Gallagher, in January of 1967, began the largest renewal and building project undertaken in the parish. The first phase of this project was the purchase of the school property. The Sisters of Charity of Nazareth, Kentucky, requested that St. Joseph's Church purchase for the Diocese of Little Rock, the Annunciation Academy property, following the trend that school properties be owned by the Parish. Bishop Fletcher approved the transaction, and the transfer of the property to the Diocese was effected on

31 December 1967. The name of the school was changed to St. Joseph's Catholic School. (See chapter 18. Annunciation Academy.)[22]

The second phase of the project was remodeling the old school building. It was decided to remodel the class rooms by removing the Sisters dining room and kitchen to the second floor, eliminating the old stage, and making this room much larger. The old cafeteria was converted into a library, with the over all cost of the project being approximately $30,000.[24]

There was a need for a new Parish Hall, and a new school cafeteria, and so it was decided to construct a multi-purpose hall and cafeteria. This was the third phase of the renewal and building project under Monsignor Gallagher. The new hall was completed in late December of 1968 at a cost of $160,000. To honor Monsignor Gallagher, the St. Joseph's Parish Board of Education adopted a resolution to name the hall, "The Right Reverend Monsignor Gallagher Hall." Gallagher Hall is equipped with stage, restrooms, closets for storage, and kitchen. It is fully air conditioned and will seat 600 people in the auditorium, and 300 for dining.[25]

The fourth phase of the overall renewal and construction project began in June of 1969. Monsignor Gallagher engaged a consulting and engineering firm to make an inspection of the church and its foundation, and they recommended that certain steps be taken to correct a moisture condition and overall deterioration of the building. The late Mr. Willard Burks, of the architectural firm of Reed-Willis and Burks was consulted, and plans were drawn for the necessary repair and renovations to the church. The work began in June of 1969, and the re-dedication ceremonies were held on Sunday, 14 December 1969. The overall cost was approximately $115,000.[26]

While the work was being done on the church, Gallagher Hall was used for a chapel for the Sunday Masses. A fund drive was conducted in the Spring of 1967, and a total amount of $145,000 was pledged—contributions to be made over a five year period. It was necessary to negotiate a bank loan to complete the cost payments. The total costs of all of these projects was more than $450,000, the largest expenditure for improvements since the parish was founded.[27] Thus the church building was given a completely new "face lifting." The exterior brick and stone was sand blasted and water proofed; new front steps were installed; a new roof replaced the old one; new gutters and down spouts; new doors added, and new pews to replace the old ones. The interior was redecorated and wall to wall carpeting replaced the old floor tile covering.[28]

The altar on which the Sacrifice of the Cross is made was placed in St. Joseph's Church under the administration of Monsignor Gallagher. It is made from the same Carrara marble used in the main altar and side altars.

Monsignor Gallagher served St. Joseph's Church from 1954 until 1972, when ill health forced him to retire. Monsignor Gallagher's death occured, 11 April 1982, Pine Bluff, Arkansas. His grave is in Graceland Cemetery, Pine Bluff.

The Most Reverend Lawrence P. Graves was assigned to St. Joseph's by Bishop Andrew J. McDonald, 3 January 1973 to June of 1973. He was appointed the Bishop of Alexandria on 22 May 1973, by His Holiness, Pope Paul VI and installed as Bishop of Alexandria, 15 October 1973.[29]

The Reverend John Francis O'Donnell was sent to St. Joseph's, Pine Bluff by the Most Reverend Andrew J. McDonald, Bishop of Little Rock, 1 July 1973. He was Coordinator for Holy Year programs, and Dean of the Southeastern Deanery, as of December 1973. Father O'Donnell, a native of Philadelphia, Pennsylvania came to St. Joseph's from St. Peter's Church, Wynne, Arkansas.[30]

While stationed in Pine Bluff, Father O'Donnell made many friends, and is well known for his ecumenical work in this city. He accomplished his purposes as he built for the future, as well as for the present, for this Parish and for the community at large. His tenure in Pine Bluff had a great influence in the community, and he is most fondly remembered by all who knew him.

In 1981, Bishop McDonald assigned Father O'Donnell to Immaculate Conception Church, North Little Rock, Arkansas.

In June of 1981, the Reverend Leo A. Riedmueller was sent to Pine Bluff by the Most Reverend Andrew J. McDonald, Bishop of Little Rock. Father Riedmueller, a native of Morrilton, Arkansas, came to St. Joseph's from St. Theresa's Church in Little Rock.

From June 1981 until the present time, St. Joseph's Parish has been fortunate indeed, to have as their Pastor, a man who has commanded the respect and admiration of all with whom he has been associated. In the summer of 1982, Bishop McDonald sent as Administrator, Father David Jacobs from Immaculate Conception, North Little Rock, and then in 1983, Father Thomas Donahue was made Associate Pastor at St. Joseph's.

Father Leo Riedmueller has dedicated his life to the service of others, and gained the true affection of all of his parishioners. With his sympathetic understanding, his warm and sincere personality and delightful sense of humor, we at St. Joseph's Church have great reason to be thankful that he is among us.

Chapter 10
Associate Pastors 1908–1984

1908	Fr. Keefe
1910	Fr. Scott
1913	Fr. Nacke
1913–1916	Fr. Norton
1925	Fr. A. Tomolunas
1925–1926	Fr. John E. Gaffney
1926	Fr. Leo Saunders
	Fr. Procipno Neuzil
1926–1927	Fr. John J. Thompson
1927–1928	Fr. Charles B. McCoy
1928	Fr. John F. Thompson
1929	Fr. Lawrence O'Neill
1929–1930	Fr. Thomas L. Keaney
1930	Fr. E. Hinckley
1931	Fr. J. F. Murphy
1932	Fr. Joseph J. Laughlin
1932–1934	Fr. R. J. McCauley
1933	Fr. C. Stanowski
1934	Fr. Casey
1936	Fr. S. F. Jacklin
1936–1937	Fr. Thomas P. Reynolds
1938–1939	Fr. F. J. Kilpatrick
1938–1941	Fr. F. X. Dollarton
1941–1942	Fr. Charles McGinnis
1942	Fr. John Mulligan
1942–1943	Fr. Charles S. Diamond

1943–1944	Fr. Jesse C. Cheney
1945–1946	Fr. William J. Burke
1946–1949	Fr. William K. Wellman
1949–1951	Fr. Francis J. Janesko
1951–1953	Fr. Ralph Bauer
1953–1954	Fr. Bernard Malone
1954–1957	Fr. John J. Kettler
1957–1958	Fr. Thomas Stauder
1957–1959	Fr. Paul McLaughlin
1959–1960	Fr. James Walters
1960–1962	Fr. Thomas W. Keller
1960–1964	Fr. Thomas Stauder
1962–1965	Fr. Robert Dienert
1965–1966	Fr. Joseph Pallo
1966–1967	Fr. Harold Luneau
1967–1968	Fr. Guy Baltz
1968–1969	Fr. Edward L. Mooney
1969–1971	Fr. James E. Mancini
1971–1973	Fr. Robert Dienert
1971–1973	Fr. Kevin McCarthy
1973–1976	Fr. Al Baltz
1976	Fr. V. E. Maguire
1976–1979	Fr. Joe Knoeber
1979–1981	Fr. Ernest Hardesty
1983	Fr. Thomas J. Donahue

Chapter 11
Memorials

Some of the memorials presently in use at St. Joseph's Church are:[1]
Three Chairs for Priests—given by the Altar Society
Holy Water Container—in grateful tribute to Sister Mary Leo, S.C.N.
The Organ—Lucey Club[2]
Papal Flag—The Altar Society
American Flag—The Altar Society
Brass Advent Wreath on Brass Standard—The Altar Society
Outdoor Flag Pole—The Catholic Daughters of the Americas
White Cope—In memory of Golden and Henry Webkes, donated by their children
Cloth on altar of Sacrifice of the Mass—The Harry Failla Family
Main Altar—In memory of the Right Reverend John M. Lucey, V.G., Pastor A.D. 1873–1914 R.I.P.
Blessed Virgin's Altar—In loving memory of Mrs. Julia Cannon died 20 October 1923 R.I.P.
St. Joseph's Altar—In loving memory of Mrs. Mary Portis
Communion Rail—This Communion Rail erected by Annie Norris Jones—In memory of her mother
The Pulpit—donated by Eulalie W. Benton—In Loving memory of her mother, Mrs. Margaret E. Benton A.D. 1939

There are doubtless many other memorials, i.e., candlesticks, candlelabra, the marble Baptismal Font, etc. which do not bear memorial name plaques, and since all records of these items seem to have vanished, this author is unable to list each and every memorial placed in the church building.

St. Joseph's Educational Fund

In 1979–1980, three of our priests, Father Ernest Hardesty, Father Michael Aureli, and Father David LeSieur became committed to the idea that the future of the church lies in our Catholic youth.[3]

To this end, they established a savings account for the purpose of a Theology Scholarship Fund, and that it should be sponsored by the Parish. The Second Vatican Council's Decree on the Apostolate of Lay People strongly speaks to the urgent necessity of men and women to become actively involved ... the purpose to advance the lay ministry within the Diocese and Parishes ... area of study could include: Theology (Moral, Christology, Sacramental), Religious Education, Church Music, Liturgical Studies, Canon Law, Youth Ministry and Scripture Studies.)[4]

The objective is to have the recipient of a scholarship return to the Diocese of Little Rock, and to use his or her knowledge for the benefit of Arkansas parishes.[5]

A trust fund was established in the parish by Mrs. Gabe Meyer as a memorial to the Cady and Meyer families and this was to become known as the St. Joseph's Educational Fund. This fund is open to receive gifts and contributions.[6]

Further memorials include the beautiful stained glass windows in St. Joseph's Church.[7]

Large windows Westside—South to North

1. In memory of Mr. & Mrs. Theo. Thessing, Sr.
2. In memory of the Missionary Priests of the Little Rock Diocese (over door—west side)
3. Mrs. Lucelia P. Jenkins and Family
4. In memory of Ben A. and Charles H. Sylvester
5. The Aureli Family
6. The Payne and Cratin Family
7. The Primo Ruggeri Family
8. In memory of Henry Kalkbrenner and Family
9. (Small window in front of church) Mr. & Mrs. F. V. De Bona

Large Windows Eastside—South to North

1. In memory of Rev. Walter J. Tynin
2. In thanksgiving—John J. Craig Family (east side over door)
3. Victory Court number 564—Catholic Daughters of America
4. In loving memory of Carl Abbene, died August 22, 1922
5. The Steele Family

6. In memory of Mr. and Mrs. George A. Conery
7. In memory of William F. and Annie Merle
8. In memory of John Boyle
9. (Small window in front of church—east side) Mr. & Mrs. Louis J. Kessel

High Windows Westside—South to North

1. The Altar Society
2. The Altar Society
3. Ivey, Armfield Family
4. The R. M. Bryant Family
5. Mr. & Mrs. Paul Finkbeiner
6. Mr. & Mrs. Paul Finkbeiner
7. In memory of Mr. & Mrs. W. H. Evans
8. Mrs. Anne Sylvester
9. In memory Charles Cook
10. In memory Theresa Cook
11. Stephen Foti Family
12. Charles Barranco Family
13. In memory of Mrs. Mary Dempsey
14. In memory Mrs. Gallagher and Dorothy
15. The John Merlo Family
16. The Kirchgraber Family

High Windows East Side—South to North

1. The H. S. Webkes Family
2. Scanlen Family
3. Mr. and Mrs. H. E. Reyer
4. The W. J. Crutcher Family
5. In memory Maas Maher Family
6. The Fred I. Maher Family
7. The Matz Family
8. The Rike Family
9. The Boswell Family
10. The Franey Family
11. Emilie M. Patterson
12. Elizabeth Boyce
13. In memory Mrs. Clara Aull
14. The Choir
15. The Ernst Family
16. The Minoret Family

High Windows in Apse of church—East to West

1. In memory of Frank P. King
2. The H. S. Webkes Family
3. In memory of Beulah Sennet
4. The W. J. Crutcher Family
5. The Cady Family
6. The Aldo Turchi Family
7. In memory of Mr. and Mrs. F. H. Brenke

Chapter 12

The Priests of St. Joseph's

History records the pastors of St. Joseph's Church prior to the year 1872, in the following order:[1]

1858–1864	Rev. P. I. Clarke from Canada
1858	Rev. P. Behan
1859–1863	Rev. Thomas Donovan
1867	Rev. Francis Laughran
1867–1868	Rev. Phillip Shanahan
1868–1872	Rev. John P. Duggan

As mentioned previously in this text, the baptismal and other records actually on hand in St. Joseph's Church, all begin with the year 1858. This is not to say that some scattered interment dates are not included, they are, but any actual record of this death is not recorded. Only information taken from the tomb stone. This writer has not been able to find any information concerning the above mentioned priests, as all of the early records, unfortunately have disappeared.

The Right Reverend Monsignor John Michael Lucey V.G.
1872–1914

The Right Reverend Monsignor John Michael Lucey was born at Troy, New York, 29 September 1843. He attended St. Andrew's College at Fort Smith, Arkansas in 1859, Ward's Academy, Fort Smith in 1860. When the Civil War broke out, he enlisted in the Confederate Army, joining the Fort Smith Rifles, Company A, 3rd Arkansas Infantry, and served throughout the Civil War.

The Right Reverend Monsignor John Michael Lucey, V.G.

After the Civil War he resumed his studies and was graduated from Fordham University in New York in 1868. He studied Theology at Mount St. Mary's Seminary, Cincinnati, Ohio for two years, then returned to Fort Smith where he was the Principal of the High School Department of the Fort Smith public schools. He was ordained in Fort Smith 14 November 1872.[2] Father Lucey became pastor of St. Joseph's Church, 21 December 1872.[3]

Father Lucey was made Domestic Prelate, or The Right Reverend Monsignòr by Pope Pius X in August of 1903. He was appointed Vicar-General of the Diocese of Little Rock by Bishop Morris in June 1907.

After a long illness, Monsignor Lucey died in San Antonio, Texas, 20 June 1914, and is buried in his family plot in Fort Smith, Arkansas.[4]

The Right Reverend Monsignor Patrick Henry Enright

The Right Reverend Monsignor Patrick Henry Enright
1914–1917

    Monsignor Patrick Henry Enright was born in 1864 in Ireland. In his early teens he began his studies in the Jesuit College at Mungreth, Ireland, where he studied for six years, after which he took a two year course in Philosophy at Maynoth Seminary. He came to the United States and completed his education for the ministry at Mount St. Mary's College near Baltimore, Maryland where he studied Theology for three years.
    On August 15, 1890 he was ordained to the priesthood at Mobile, Alabama. Father Enright's first parish was at Grady, Arkansas. Next he was sent to Little Rock, and then made assistant to the Very Reverend Bishop John B. Morris. In August of 1914, the Reverend Patrick H. Enright was sent to St. Joseph's, Pine Bluff, and in January of 1915, he was elevated to Monsignor.

Monsignor Enright died suddenly in Hot Springs, Arkansas 10 April 1917.[5]

The Reverend Patrick J. Higgins
1917–1922

Father Patrick J. Higgins was born in County Roscommon, Ireland, town of Boyle in 1877. He was ordained in 1910 by Bishop John B. Morris, Bishop of Little Rock.[6]

Father Higgins served at St. Andrew's Cathedral, Little Rock, Our Lady of Hope Church, Hope, Arkansas, St. Mary's Church, Helena, Arkansas, and St. Joseph's Church, Pine Bluff. He returned to Ireland where he stayed for several years; his health at this time was poor.[7]

Father Higgins died in a New Orleans hospital in 1950 and the Solemn Requiem Funeral Mass was held in the chapel of St. John's Seminary with Bishop Fletcher and Monsignor Thomas L. Keany, a relative of Father Higgins, as celebrants of the Mass, assisted by many priests and seminarians at St. John's.[8]

The Very Reverend Monsignor Walter J. Tynin
1922–1930

Father Walter J. Tynin was born in Jonesboro, Arkansas, 13 February 1888, a son of Thomas A. Tynin and Amanda Jane Land. Father Tynin attended the parish school of Jonesboro and Pocahontas, Arkansas, and later enrolled in Subiaco High School and College from which he received his A. M. degree.[9] He decided to study for the priesthood, and applied to Bishop Morris for adoption as a clerical student of the Diocese. He was received by the Bishop and was sent by him to the American College in Rome, Italy, being the first native Arkansan to study for the Diocese of Little Rock. He entered the American College in Rome on the 18th of October 1906; studied Philosophy, two years, Theology, three years, and received minor degrees in these subjects. He was awarded the minor orders and sub-diaconate in Rome, and returned to Arkansas, being ordained deacon priest by the Right Reverend John B. Morris, on the 17th and 18th of October 1911.[10]

He was first assigned as assistant at St. John's, Hot Springs, later stationed in Atkins, St. John's Seminary at Little Rock, Fayetteville, Blessed Sacrament, Jonesboro and appointed to St. Joseph's, Pine Bluff in April 1922,[11] and Holy Redeemer, El Dorado.

Father Tynin died at St. Vincent's Infirmary, Little Rock, following a long illness. A Pontifical Funeral Mass of Requiem was celebrated 23 November 1948 at Blessed Sacrament Church, Jonesboro by His

The Very Reverend Monsignor Walter J. Tynin

Excellency Bishop Fletcher. Burial was in Blessed Sacrament Cemetery, Jonesboro, Arkansas.[12]

The Very Reverend Gregory H. Keller
1930–1940

Father Keller was born in Little Rock, 24 May 1895, son of Professor and Mrs. Joseph Keller. His father was organist and choir director of St. Andrew's Cathedral for more than 50 years. Father Keller received his elementary education at St. Andrew's Cathedral School. He completed eight grades of Grammar School in six years, and in 1908 enrolled in the Freshman class of the High School Department of Little Rock College, which Bishop Morris had founded that year. He completed the four years High School course in three years, and was Valedictorian of his class. He

The Very Reverend Gregory H. Keller

continued his studies at Little Rock College, and was awarded a Bachelor of Arts degree in 1913. He then was sent to Rome where he studied Theology for six years at the Propaganda de Fide University.[13]

Father Keller was ordained in Rome, 15 March 1919 by the late Cardinal Pompili, and when he returned to Arkansas, he was assigned to the faculty of St. John's Seminary.[14]

In 1923 he was assigned to Sts. Cyril and Methodius Church at Slovactown, Arkansas, 1924 to Holy Redeemer, El Dorado, and 1930 to St. Joseph's, Pine Bluff.[15]

In 1940 he was assigned to St. Mary's Church, Helena, 1954 to St. Patrick's Church in Little Rock, and in 1958 to St. Paul's Church, Pocahontas, Arkansas.[16]

Father Keller died in Alabama 28 September 1979, and a Mass of Christian Burial was offered at St. Bernard's Abbey, St. Bernard, Alabama.

The Very Reverend Monsignor Thomas Francis Walshe

At the time of his death, he was the oldest priest in the Little Rock Diocesan clergy.[17]

Father Keller's reputation as an inventor grew with the years. It began as a hobby, and at his death, he held patents on machines for decorating candy, for packaging salted peanuts, and processing peanut butter cracker sandwiches. These labor saving devices became his interest because his late brother-in-law, Bob McCormack owned Bob's Candies in Albany, Georgia. Many charities benefited financially from royalties Father Keller received from his inventions.[18]

The Very Reverend Monsignor Thomas Francis Walshe
1940–1954

The Very Reverend Monsignor Thomas Francis Walshe was born in San

Francisco, California, 3 July 1901. He attended St. James Parochial School at San Francisco, and St. Patrick's Seminary at Menlo Park, California.[19]

He came to Little Rock to enter St. John's Home Missions Seminary in the fall of 1921. He was ordained by Bishop John B. Morris, 1 November 1925 in St. Andrew's Cathedral, Little Rock.[20]

His first assignment was that of an assistant at St. Andrew's Cathedral, where he served for about three years. In 1928 he went to Forest City, Arkansas where he was an assistant at St. Francis Mission House, remaining there for the next two years.[21]

In 1930 he was appointed pastor of St. Joseph's Church at Fayetteville with the care of St. Joseph's Mission Church at Tonitown. He went to El Dorado as pastor of Holy Redeemer parish in 1933, and served this parish for seven years.[22]

The next 14 years he spent at Pine Bluff as Pastor of St. Joseph's Church, to which he was appointed in 1940. While there, he became Dean of the Southeast Deanery on 26 July 1948. He went to Fort Smith, 1 September 1954 as pastor of Immaculate Conception parish, at which time he was appointed Dean of the Northwest Deanery.[23]

Monsignor Walshe was the son of Alice and Martin Walshe of San Francisco. He died Wednesday, 5 October 1966 in Fort Smith, Arkansas. Funeral mass was held at Immaculate Conception Church, and burial was in Calvary Cemetery in Fort Smith.[24]

The Right Reverend Monsignor Joseph A. Gallagher
1954–1972

Monsignor Gallagher was born in Philadelphia, Pennsylvania, 5 May 1896. His early education was obtained at Philadelphia schools, Mount Carmel and Epiphany parochial schools, and Roman Catholic High School. After graduation he attended Holy Ghost Preparatory College and Temple University.[25]

Monsignor Gallagher came to Little Rock in 1920 and enrolled at St. John's Home Missions Seminary. He was ordained 21 May 1925 in St. Andrew's Cathedral by Bishop John B. Morris.[26]

His first appointment was to the faculty of St. John's Seminary, where he remained for the next 20 years. He became the seminary's vice-rector in 1932.[27]

While at the seminary, he was also Director of Vocations, and spent the summers in Philadelphia and the East, enlisting vocations for the mission diocese. Many of the Diocese's priests today, came to Little Rock from Philadelphia and the East upon the suggestion and encouragement of Monsignor Gallagher.[28]

He was appointed Papal Chamberlain with the title of Very Reverend

The Right Reverend Monsignor Joseph A. Gallagher

Monsignor in 1934, and raised to the rank of Domestic Prelate with the title of Right Reverend Monsignor in 1942.[29]

In January 1945 he was appointed pastor of Christ the King parish in Fort Smith, and in August 1947 he became pastor of Immaculate Conception, Fort Smith. He was assigned pastor of St. Joseph's Church, Pine Bluff in September of 1954, and Dean of the Southeast Deanery.[30]

Monsignor Gallagher died 11 April 1982 in Pine Bluff and his grave is in Graceland Cemetery, Pine Bluff.[31]

The Most Reverend Lawrence Preston Graves, D.D.
1972–1973

Bishop Lawrence Preston Graves was born 4 May 1916, Texarkana, Arkansas. He received his elementary and high school education at St.

The Most Reverend Lawrence Preston Graves, D.D.

Edward's Parochial School and Providence Academy in Texarkana.[32]

He began studies for the priesthood in 1934 when he entered St. John's Home Missions Seminary in Little Rock. Two years later he was sent to the North American College in Rome by Bishop John B. Morris. After four years of study at Gregorian University there, he was forced to return to this country in 1940 because of World War II. He completed his studies at St. John's and was ordained 11 June 1942 by Bishop Morris in St. Andrew's Cathedral in Little Rock.[33]

His first appointment was as assistant pastor of Immaculate Conception Church, Fort Smith in 1942, then Professor, St. John's Seminary, Little Rock 1943, and then he was sent to Catholic University, Washington, D.C. in 1945, for advanced studies in Canon Law, then the Faculty, Catholic High School Little Rock in 1947, made Vice-Chancellor 1947, then Officialis of the Diocesan Tribunal, Little Rock in 1955.[34]

The Reverend John Francis O'Donnell

In 1958 he was in residence at St. Patrick's Church rectory, North Little Rock, then Papal Chamberlain 1961, Auxiliary Bishop of Little Rock, 25 April 1969, Vice General and Consultor 1969, reappointed Auxiliary Bishop 1972, then pastor of St. Joseph's Church, Pine Bluff and Dean of the Southeastern Deanery, 2 January 1973.[35]

On 22 May 1973, he was appointed Bishop of Alexandria by His Holiness, Pope Paul VI. He was installed as Bishop of Alexandria, 15 October 1973. Bishop Graves retired 20 July 1982.

The Very Reverend John Francis O'Donnell
1973–1981

Father John Francis O'Donnell was born in Philadelphia, Pennsylvania 29 January 1928, a son of Bridget and Henry O'Donnell. He attended parochial school in his home parish of The Seven Dolors, and graduated from Northeast Catholic High School in Philadelphia.[37]

Father O'Donnell came to Little Rock in the fall of 1946 to enter St. John's Home Missions Seminary. He was ordained by His Excellency, Bishop Albert L. Fletcher on 27 May 1954.[38]

His first assignment was as assistant pastor of St. John's parish in Hot Springs. A year later he was appointed to the faculty of Catholic High School in Little Rock where he taught for the next five years. In 1960 he was made assistant pastor of Our Lady of the Holy Souls Parish in Little Rock, and was also moderator of the Senior Catholic Youth Organization of Greater Little Rock.[39]

In August of 1965, Father O'Donnell was made pastor of Holy Cross Church, Crossett, Arkansas, in September of 1969, pastor of St. Peter's Church, Wynne, Arkansas, and appointed a member of the Diocesan Personnel Board in December of 1972.[40]

Father O'Donnell became pastor of St. Joseph's Church, Pine Bluff in July of 1973 and was Coordinator for Holy Year programs, and Dean of the Southeastern Deanery in October of 1973. In June of 1981, Father O'Donnell was assigned as pastor of Immaculate Conception Church, North Little Rock, Arkansas where he is serving at the present time.

The Very Reverend Leo Anthony Riedmueller, V.F.
1981

The Very Reverend Leo Anthony Riedmueller was born 14 January 1924 in Morrilton, Arkansas, a son of Elizabeth Laux and George W. Riedmueller.[41]

Father Riedmueller attended Sacred Heart Church in Morrilton and all 12 grades of school at Sacred Heart School in Morrilton, from which he graduated in 1941.[42]

He studied at St. John's Home Missions Seminary in Little Rock, and was ordained to the priesthood on 22 May 1948 by Bishop Albert L. Fletcher in St. Andrew's Cathedral, Little Rock.[43]

Father Riedmueller was appointed to the faculty of Catholic High School, 21 June 1948, where he taught for 17 years. He was in 1954, Chaplain at St. Vincent's Infirmary, Little Rock, Chaplain of Our Lady of Nazareth Home, Little Rock, Chaplain at St. Joseph's Orphanage in 1964, Spiritual Director at St. John's Seminary, Little Rock in 1965, and appointed to the faculty of Mount St. Mary's Academy, Little Rock. While teaching, he served at St. Andrew's Cathedral, Little Rock, St. Patrick's Church in North Little Rock, and Immaculate Conception Church in North Little Rock.[44]

Father Riedmueller was made Administrator of St. Edward's Church, Texarkana in July of 1967, Pastor of St. Edward's in September 1967, Pastor

The Very Reverend Leo Anthony Riedmueller, V.F. Photography by Lites Studio—John Doll, Jr.

of St. Joseph's Church, Fayetteville, Arkansas in July of 1973. He was then assigned as Pastor of St. Theresa's Church, Little Rock in August of 1975, and made Dean of the Little Rock Deanery 23 June 1976 for three years. He was Spiritual Moderator Diocesan Council of Catholic Men in March of 1976, and appointed to the Clergy Personnel Board for 3 years in December of 1976.[45]

On 6 June 1981, Father Riedmueller was assigned as our Pastor at St. Joseph's Church, Pine Bluff, and made Dean of the Southeastern Deanery for 3 years, in July of 1981.[46]

Chapter 13
The Sisters of St. Joseph's

A 350-year-old tradition is alive and well in Pine Bluff. For the past 350 years, a Catholic order of sisters has been fulfilling its commitment and members of the order continue that commitment today in Pine Bluff.[1]

The Daughters of Charity of Saint Vincent de Paul was formed in France in 1633. The Daughters of Charity total about 38,000 world wide. The Motherhouse is located in Paris; their provincial house in St. Louis, Missouri. Among their particular interests are aiding the elderly, the sick, youth and the poor. Each of the sisters is a well-trained and well educated professional, drawing from a legacy of experience in social work and religious instruction.[2] But more than that, they have given their lives to God and want their work to be recognized as a privilege and a blessing bestowed on them by their dedication to their faith.[3]

The Sisters presently serving in Pine Bluff are:

Sister Jane Frances Bey, photographed in Cornette and long Habit. This Habit used by the Daughters of Charity until approximately 1964.

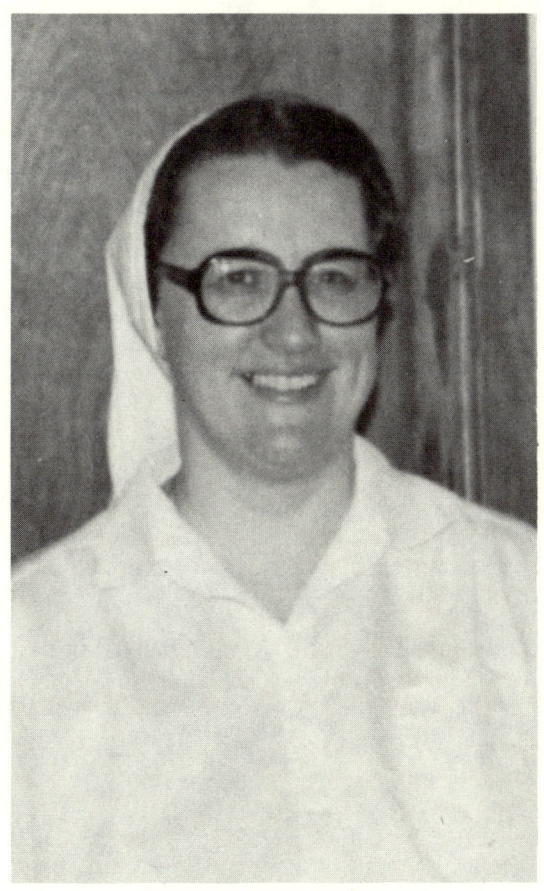

Sister Patricia Bachman

Sister Patricia Bachman

Sister Patricia Bachman was born in Kansas City, Missouri. She met the Daughters of Charity while working part time at Pius X Boarding Home for Children. In August of 1966 she entered the Daughters of Charity as a postulant. From 1969–1975 and 1981–1982 she was housemother at St. Elizabeth's Home for Girls in New Orleans.[8]

In 1975–1981 she worked in San Antonio, Texas in a Medical, Dental and Social Service Agency, De Paul Family Center. In 1982, Sister Patricia spent 1 year in the Diocese of Lincoln, Nebraska setting up a program for mentally retarded adults, and in 1983 she came to Pine Bluff, to work in The Helping Hand Office of the Catholic Social Services and to assist, where needed, in St. Peter's Parish, Pine Bluff.[9]

Sister Jane Frances Bey

Sister Jane Frances Bey

Sister Jane Frances Bey was born in Perryville, Missouri. After 12 years of being educated by the Daughters of Charity, she entered that community in 1928. One year later she was missioned to Charity Hospital in New Orleans. There she earned a degree in nursing and is a registered nurse, fulfilling 21 years of dedicated service. Sister Jane Frances in the years following, gave her life to God's people through Social Ministry in Texas, Louisiana, Illinois, Indiana and in Fort Smith, Arkansas.

Sister Mary Catherine Dunn

Sister Mary Catherine Dunn was born in St. Louis, Missouri. In 1961 she entered the Daughters of Charity and was asked to pursue a degree in

Sister Mary Catherine Dunn

Dietetics. This she did, and received her degree in 1967 from Fontbonne College in St. Louis, and then studied in Cincinnati for a 1 year internship program. For 10 years, she worked as an administrative dietitian in nursing homes, and general and psychiatric hospitals in Mobile, New Orleans and St. Louis. Sister Mary Catherine received her undergraduate degree in Social Work from the University of Texas at Arlington. She established the diocesan office of Catholic Social Services and The Helping Hand in Pine Bluff, a volunteer agency which helps poor families.[5]

Sister Stephanie Hudek

Sister Stephanie Hudek was born in Weimer, Texas. On 21 June 1924 she entered the Community of the Daughters of Charity. Throughout her Religious life, Sister Stephanie has ministered as a dietitian for community

Sister Stephanie Hudek

hospitals and schools in Missouri, Utah and California. Sister Stephanie served in Fort Smith, Arkansas for five years and is involved in the ministry of Evangelization through home visiting throughout the area, and periodic visits at the Women's Prison Unit. Sister Stephanie is an excellent cook for the Sisters and is very talented in vegetable and flower gardening.[6]

Sister Maria Kleinschmidt

Sister Maria Kleinschmidt was born in Winona, Minnesota. In the autumn of 1963 she became a Daughter of Charity. She received a Bachelors degree in Theology and for several years was involved in parish life by teaching religion in grades, one through twelve. In 1977 she completed graduate work at St. Louis University, and received a Masters degree in Theology. Sister Maria has served in Alabama, Missouri and

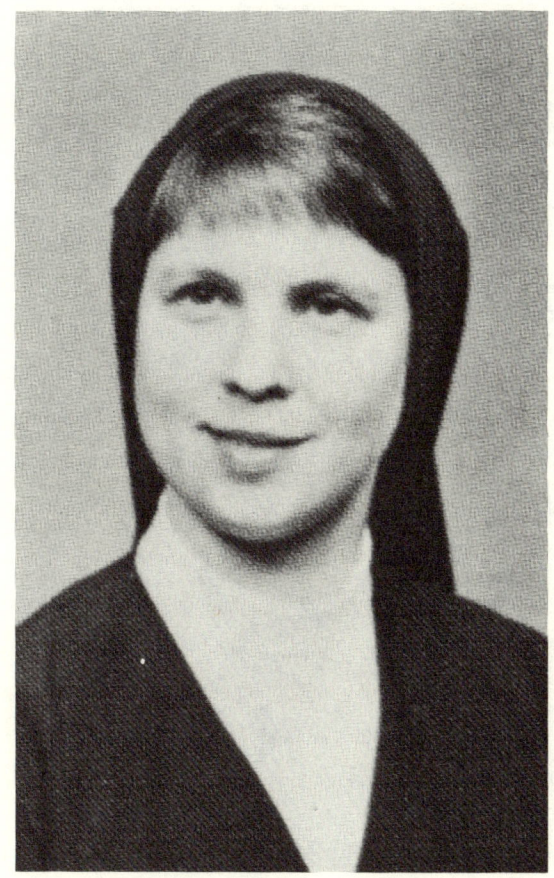

Sister Maria Kleinschmidt

Louisiana and has had education and experience in the areas of Religious Education, Parish Ministry, Liturgy and Spiritual Counseling.[7]

Mr. Frank Velvin King

Chapter 14
The Deacons of St. Joseph's

His Excellency Bishop Andrew J. McDonald, D.D. celebrated the Eucharist of Ordination of Permanent Deans for the Diocese of Little Rock, 7 November 1981 at the Cathedral of St. Andrew at Little Rock.[1]

Three men from St. Joseph's Church, Pine Bluff were ordained permanent deacons on that day. The ordination was an historic event because it was the ordination of the first class of permanent deacons who have received their formation in the Diocese of Little Rock.[2]

These men are no longer lay persons, but became members of the clergy, although they continue living the life of a lay person in their responsibilities to their family and their secular employment. The most visible role of the deacon is at Mass, as they assist the priest, proclaim the Gospel, prepare the Altar and distribute Communion. They are also able to baptize, witness marriages and conduct funerals.[3]

Frank Velvin (Buddy) King

A native of Pine Bluff, Buddy King attended Little Rock University and Memphis State University. He serves as president of Apache Van Lines, Inc. and City Delivery, Inc. and is active in the Kiwanis Club of Pine Bluff.[4]

Mr. King served as president of the Arkansas Household Goods Carriers Bureau and served on the executive committees of Arkansas Bus and Truck Association and Arkansas Movers Association.

He and his wife Judy are the parents of Kevin King, Carmen King and and the late Curtis King. He has chosen as his ministry, the Arkansas Prison System.[5]

Mr. Donald B. Lynch

Donald B. Lynch

Mr. Lynch has been a resident of Pine Bluff since 1949, and is a native of Minneapolis, Minnesota. After receiving a bachelor's degree in Forestry from the University of Minnesota, he worked as a forester for the United States Soil Conservation Service. In 1942, he joined Joseph E. Seagram and Son, Inc. and remained with them in the cooperage division in various capacities until his retirement in 1977.[6]

He and the late Mrs. Lynch have three daughters: Mrs. James Moore of Palo Alto, California, Sister Donald Mary, R.S.M. of St. Louis, Missouri, and Mrs. Vernon Kidd of Dallas, Texas, and four grandchildren.[7]

Mr. Tim Massanelli

Tim Massanelli

Mr. Tim Massanelli is a life long resident of Pine Bluff. He attended Annunciation Academy and Pine Bluff High School and Drury College at Springfield, Missouri.[8]

He serves as president of Wilcox Amusement Company, vice-president of Holsum Baking Company, and is on the board of directors at First South Federal Savings and Loan Association, and a member of the Board of Directors of Jefferson Regional Medical Center.[9]

Active in political affairs of the community and state, Mr. Massanelli is parliamentarian of the Arkansas House of Representatives and is administrative assistant to the Speaker of the House.[10]

He is married to the former Dottie Walters of Pine Bluff, and they are the parents of three sons.

The Reverend Michael Valentine Aureli

Chapter 15

The Priests from St. Joseph's

The Reverend Michael Valentine Aureli son of Mr. Al Aureli and the late Mrs. Aureli was born in Pine Bluff, Arkansas 14 February 1950. He attended Annunciation Academy, Pine Bluff, Dial Junior High School, Pine Bluff, and Pine Bluff High School. He studied four years at the University of Dallas, four years at Branniff Graduate School (University of Dallas) Holy Trinity Seminary. He holds a B.A. in Philosophy, and Masters of Divinity in Theology.[1]

He was ordained to the Priesthood, 22 May 1976, at St. Joseph's Church, Pine Bluff by His Excellency, Bishop Andrew J. McDonald, Bishop of Little Rock.[2]

The Reverend Albert C. Ernst J.C.D. son of the late Mr. & Mrs. Albert C. Ernst of Pine Bluff, was born in Shreveport, Louisiana 18 July 1926. He was the first young man from St. Joseph's Parish to be ordained to the Priesthood.

He received his elementary education at Annunciation Academy, Pine Bluff, and his high school education at Pine Bluff High School. In 1944 he joined the United States Naval Air Corps and subsequently attended the University of Southern California at Los Angeles and Loyola University at New Orleans. He entered St. John's Seminary in 1948 and was ordained by His Excellency, Bishop Albert L. Fletcher, 30 May 1953.[3]

The Reverend Frederick Walter Gunti son of the late Mr. Frederick Walter Gunti and Mattie Maude Lovelady Gunti, was born 13 July 1940 at Memphis, Tennessee. He attended Annunciation Academy, Pine Bluff for nine grades of school, and St. John's Seminary, Little Rock for seven years, three years of high school and four of college. He studied at the Pontifical Gregorian University, Rome, Italy for four years. He holds a Bachelor of Arts

The Reverend Albert C. Ernst

from St. John's Seminary, Bachelor of Sacred Theology, Pontifical Gregorian University, Licentiate in Sacred Theology, Pontifical Gregorian University.[4]

Father Gunti was ordained to the Priesthood in St. Peter's Basilica, Vatican City State by the Most Reverend Francis F. Reh, STL, JCD on 16 December 1964.[5]

The Reverend Charles David LeSieur son of Mr. & Mrs. Charles LeSieur was born 29 March 1950 at Jackson, Mississippi. He attended St. Edward's, Texarkana, Arkansas for half a year, Annunciation Academy, Pine Bluff for seven and a half years, Catholic High School, Little Rock for four years, University of Dallas for five years, and St. Meinrad School of Theology for three years. He holds a B.A. in Humanities and a Master of Divinity.[6]

He was ordained to the Priesthood, 11 December 1976 in St. Joseph's Church, Pine Bluff by His Excellency, Bishop Andrew J. McDonald, Bishop

The Reverend Frederick Walter Gunti

of Little Rock.

The Reverend Raymond Rickels O.F.M. son of Beth Ross and Charles Rickels was born in Pine Bluff, Arkansas, 28 July 1949. He graduated from Whitehall High School, Pine Bluff, and received a B.A. from the University of Arkansas at Fayetteville. He entered the Peace Corps in 1971 where he served for three years. He attended the Seminary of Our Lady of the Angels, Quincy, Illinois; a Novitiate at Oak Brook Priory, Oak Brook, Illinois.

Father Rickels has been a member of the Sacred Heart Province of the Order of Friars Minor since 1976. He made his solemn profession 11 October 1980 and was ordained to the Priesthood 5 June 1982 by the Most Reverend Jude Prost O.E.M., D.D. Father Rickels is a member of the Franciscan Order.[7]

The Reverend James P. Scull, S.J. was born 12 February 1927, son of

The Reverend Charles David LeSieur

Kathleen Rose McCauley and Ben H. Scull. His early schooling was at Sacred Heart School, Morrilton, Arkansas. He attended Creighton Preparatory School, then Creighton University.

Father Sculll studied four years in Rome at the Jesuit College where he received a Doctorate, then in Germany where he studied the German language. He taught at Marquette College, Milwaukee, Wisconsin for eight years.

Father Scull entered the Society of Jesus 4 February 1945, he was ordained 18 June 1958 by Bishop Edward J. Hunkeler. Father Scull is a Professor at Creighton Univerisity, Omaha, Nebraska.[8]

The Reverend Robert A. Torres was born 13 November 1940, son of Mrs. Trinidad Torres and the late Mr. Torres. He attended Annunciation Academy, Pine Bluff for nine years, and holds a B.A. from St. John's Seminary, Little Rock, which he attended for 11 years.

The Reverend Raymond Rickels, O.F.M.

Father Torres was ordained to the Priesthood 28 May 1966 by Bishop Albert L. Fletcher.[9]

The Reverend James P. Scull, S.J.

The Reverend Robert A. Torres

Sister Charles Teresa, S.C.N.

Chapter 16

The Sisters from St. Joseph's

Sister Adelaide Pendleton S.C.N. (Fannie Moore) was born at Crab Orchard Springs, Kentucky, 3 September 1854, daughter of Adeline Farrelly and James Harlan Moore. A communicant of St. Joseph's, she was married for 22 years to Dr. Plesant H. Pendleton of Pine Bluff and after his death, 26 March 1899, entered the Sisters of Charity of Nazareth, Kentucky, 13 August 1900, final vows 19 March 1902. Sister Adelaide died in May of 1933 and is buried in Nazareth, Kentucky.[1]

Sister Charles Teresa S.C.N. (Leona Kraeszig) daughter of the late Mr. and Mrs. Fred Kraeszig of Pine Bluff. Sister Charles Teresa received her early education at Annunciation Academy, Pine Bluff, and entered the Novitiate of the Sisters of Charity of Nazareth, Kentucky on 24 September 1948, and took her final vows on 19 July 1954.[2]

Sister Donald Mary Lynch R.S.M. (Charlotte Lynch) daughter of Mr. Donald Lynch and the late Mary Lynch of Pine Bluff. She received her early education at Annunciation Academy, Pine Bluff and graduated from Mount St. Mary's in Little Rock and entered the Novitiate of the Religious Sisters of Mercy at Our Lady of Mercy Convent, St. Louis, Missouri, 8 September 1961. She took her final vows 16 August 1969.[3]

Sister Mary Casimer S.C.N. (Annie J. Hopkins) was born 3 December 1870 in Pine Bluff, daughter of Mary Elizabeth Finnegan and Thomas Roland Hopkins. She was a pupil at Annunciation Academy, Pine Bluff and entered the Sisters of Charity of Nazareth, Nazareth, Kentucky 29 August 1888, and made her final vows, 25 March 1911. Sister Mary Casimer died at the Motherhouse, Nazareth, Kentucky 10 May 1951.[4]

Sister Mary Sylvan Tarver S.C.N. was born 6 November 1895 at Memphis, Tennessee, daughter of Rose Moore and John W. Tarver. She

Sister Donald Mary, R.S.M.

entered the Sisters of Charity of Nazareth Community 4 May 1917 from Pine Bluff. She made her perpetual vows in 1922. She died at Bardstown, Kentucky 6 November 1961, and is buried at Nazareth, Kentucky.[5]

Chapter 17

The Bishops of Little Rock

The Most Reverend Andrew Byrne, D.D.
1843–1862

The Most Reverend Andrew Byrne, D.D. the first Bishop of Little Rock, was born at Navan, Ireland, 5 December 1802. In 1820 while pursuing his studies at the Diocesan Seminary of Navan, he volunteered to go with Bishop England to Charleston, South Carolina, where he was ordained, 11 November 1827. In 1830 he was pastor of St. Mary's Church, Charleston, and was for several years the Vicar General of Bishop England, and his Theologian in 1833 at the Second Provincial Council of Baltimore. His next mission was St. James, New York City, Church of the Nativity, New York City and St. Andrew's, New York.[1]

The new Diocese of Little Rock, comprising the State of Arkansas and the Indian Territory was created in 1843. On 10 March 1844 in St. Patrick's Cathedral, New York City, Bishop Hughes as consecrating Prelate, assisted by Bishop Fenwick of Boston and Bishop Whelan of Richmond, Virginia, consecrated The Most Reverend John McClosky, Bishop of Albany; The Most Reverend William Quartier, Bishop of Chicago and the Most Reverend Andrew Byrne as Bishop of Little Rock.[2]

Bishop Andrew Byrne, our first Bishop served from 28 November 1843 until 10 June 1862. He died 10 June 1862 at Helena, Arkansas and was buried in the Sisters garden. On 20 November 1881 his body was re-interred in a crypt beneath the sanctuary of the then new St. Andrew's Cathedral, Little Rock. The Pontifical Mass was celebrated by Bishop Fitzgerald, Father McGowan, assistant priest, Father Phelan, deacon and Father D. A. Quinn as subdeacon.[3]

The Most Reverend Andrew Byrne, D.D.

The Most Reverend Edward Fitzgerald, D.D.
1866–1907

The Diocese of Little Rock had been "sede Vacante" from 18 June 1862, when Bishop Andrew Byrne died at Helena, until 22 June 1866. After the close of the Civil War, the Holy See deemed the time opportune to provide for the diocese, and the choice fell upon the Reverend Edward Fitzgerald. He was born in 1833 in Limerick, the historic city of Ireland's broken treaty.

In 1850 he pursued his studies at the Seminary of the Barrens, Perry County, Missouri. In 1852 he was a student at Mount St. Mary's of the West, Cincinnati, Ohio, and in 1855 he entered Mount St. Mary's, Emmittsburg, Maryland. He received the Holy Orders of the Priesthood, 22 August 1857, at the hands of his chosen, Bishop, Archbishop J. B. Purcell, by whom he was assigned a parish in Columbus, Ohio. This was his only mission as a priest.[4]

Bishop Fitzgerald was at the time of his consecration, the youngest Bishop in the United States.[5] This consecration took place in St. Patrick's Church, Columbus, Ohio, 3 February 1867, Archbishop Purcell being the consecrating prelate.[6]

Although the Civil War was by 1867, a thing of the past, its dreadful horrors lingered in many shapes; in mutual distrust, in lawlessness, and in the wholesale and serious depreciation of the value of property. The blundering made of reconstruction which was adopted by the United States government, deepened the wounds of public feeling, and almost obliterated all hope of permanent reconciliation. The native Catholics (of Arkansas) were not merely impoverished, but disheartened. Although settlers from the Northern and Eastern parts of the United States began to come slowly into Arkansas, few of them were Catholics. The population of the state, black and white in 1870 was 484,481 people.[7]

Conscious of the difficulties of the situation, Bishop Fitzgerald in selecting Religious Orders for the work of the state, chose those who manifestly practiced poverty, not only in spirit, but in deed; The Order of St. Benedict and The Order of the Holy Ghost, two distinct communities of Benedictine Sisters; the Sisters of Charity of Nazareth, Kentucky and the Sisters of Mercy from St. Louis.[8]

Bishop Fitzgerald had an unusually long reign of 41 years. During that time, he enjoyed the rare honor of taking part in a General Council of the Church. He was one of the Fathers of the Vatican Council in 1870.[9]

Towards the latter part of the seventies, the time was ripe for a new Cathedral. The Cathedral, at Center and Second Streets, Little Rock, erected by Bishop Byrne in 1845, was too small in 1867 for the congregation. In 1874, the Brooks and Baxter contest for the governorship, threatened to embroil the people of the State in an interminable trouble.

These events and their natural concomitants, paralyzed business and will explain why the State did not begin to advance in material prosperity until about 1878.[10]

The cornestone of the new Cathedral, Seventh and Louisiana Streets, Little Rock, was laid on 7 July 1878 by Bishop Fitzgerald.[11]

In 1900 Bishop Fitzgerald suffered a stroke which partially disabled him for active duties, and as the years passed, and the hope of his recovery dwindled away, Bishop Fitzgerald in 1906 asked for a coadjutor. Rome approved his request, and the choice fell on the Right Reverend Monsignor John Baptist Morris, Vicar General of Nashville, Tennessee.[12]

Bishop Fitzgerald died at Hot Springs, Arkansas on 21 February 1907.[13]

The Most Reverend John Baptist Morris, D.D.
1907–1946

The Most Reverend John Baptist Morris, the third Bishop of Little Rock, was born 29 June 1866 at Hendersonville, Sumner County, Tennessee. His father, John Morris was born in 1825 near Athenry, Galway County, Ireland and had emigrated to America. Bishop Morris' mother was a native of Munfordsville, Hart County, Kentucky.[14]

Bishop Morris enrolled in 1882 at St. Mary's College, Lebanon, Kentucky. After graduation he resided at the North American College in Rome and attended the Urban College De Propaganda Fide. On 11 June 1892 he was ordained to the Priesthood in the Lateran Basilica in Rome.[15]

Bishop Morris began his missionary labors at Nashville, Tennessee and in June of 1895 he was made Rector of the Cathedral, then Vicar General in 1900 and Monsignor in December of the same year.[16]

As mentioned previously, Bishop Morris was named Coadjutor—Bishop to the Most Reverend Edward Fitzgerald, Bishop of Little Rock in 1906. By the death of Bishop Fitzgerald in 1907, Bishop Morris succeeded ipso facto to the See of Little Rock.[17]

Bishop Morris brought several new religious communities into the Diocese, and among them were the Sisters of the Good Shepherd. The Catholic Publication Company was organized in 1911, the Bishop being the main share holder, which meant that he assumed the principal burden of launching the paper. The first number of the diocesan organ, The Guardian, appeared 25 March 1911.[18]

Bishop Morris conceived and carried out plans for a home institution for the education of his clergy. St. John's Home Missions Seminary was opened in Fitzgerald Hall of Little Rock College, 19 September 1911 with ten seminarians who had been studying for the diocese in other seminaries.[19]

St. Joseph's Orphanage was completed under the direction of Bishop

The Most Reverend Edward Fitzgerald, D.D.

Morris, as well as Little Rock College. In 1920, the Bishop invited the Poor Brothers of St. Francis to begin work in his diocese, and they accepted and opened Morris Institute, Armstrong Springs, 20 January 1921, and in 1920, St. Vincent's Infirmary, Little Rock, was declared by the American College of Surgeons, to be the only Class A hospital in the State of Arkansas.[20] In 1930 Bishop Morris founded Catholic High School enrolling its teachers from among the clergy.[21]

Bishop Morris died 22 October 1946 in Little Rock.[22]

The Most Reverend Albert Lewis Fletcher, D.D
1947–1972

The Most Reverend Albert Lewis Fletcher, the fourth Bishop of Little Rock was born 28 October 1896 at Little Rock, son of Helen Wehr and Dr. Thomas M. Fletcher. He attended a parochial school in Paris, Arkansas where his family was living at the time, and completed his elementary education under the Religious Sisters of Mercy at Tonitown, Arkansas.[23]

At Little Rock College he completed a high school and college course and in 1917 entered St. John's Seminary, and was ordained a priest 4 June 1920.[24]

After his ordination, Bishop Fletcher did theological work at St. John's Seminary and taught chemistry and biology at Little Rock College. He also studied at the University of Chicago and subsequently received an honorary Doctor of Philosophy degree from St. Thomas College of Milwaukee.[25]

In 1923 he was named president of Little Rock College and Vice Chancellor of the Diocese in 1925 and a year later, Chancellor. In 1933 he became Vicar General of the Diocese.[26]

Bishop Fletcher was named Monsignor by Bishop Morris, and 11 December 1939, Pope Pius XII appointed him as titular bishop of Samos—an Agean island south of Smyrna on Turkey's west coast—and auxilliary bishop of Little Rock.[27]

Bishop Morris died 22 October 1946 and the next day Bishop Fletcher was named administrative head of the Diocese. In December 1946 Pope Pius relieved him of the Samos titularship and designated him as Bishop of Little Rock. His solemn enthronement was on 11 February 1947 and he served until his resignation which was announced by the Vatican in July of 1972.[28]

Bishop Fletcher loved outdoor pastimes, especially fishing and gardening. A number of years ago when he lived at St. John's at 2500 North Tyler Street, Little Rock, he cultivated a vegetable garden on an acre near there, and kept a plow horse, Nellie. He once smilingly laid claim to being an expert plowman. After he moved to the house on Crestwood in Little Rock

The Most Reverend John Baptist Morris, D.D.

he turned to shrubbery and flowers—notably azaleas and camellias. He called his yard, "Fletcher's Wilderness," and always showed his visitors his garden "rain gauge," which was a coffee can.[29]

Bishop Fletcher died 6 December 1979, having been succeeded at his retirement in 1972 by then Right Reverend Monsignor Andrew J. McDonald who had been vicar general of the Diocese of Savannah, Georgia.[30]

The Most Reverend Andrew J. McDonald, D.D.
1972

The Most Reverend Andrew J. McDonald, D.D., the fifth Bishop of Little Rock. Bishop McDonald was born in Savannah, Georgia 24 October 1923. He graduated in 1948 from St. Mary's Seminary and the University of Baltimore, Baltimore, Maryland. He was ordained to the Priesthood 9 May 1948 at the Cathedral of St. John the Baptist, Savannah, Georgia.[31]

In 1952, Bishop McDonald received a Doctor of Canon Law degree at Lateran University, Rome, Italy and the same year was assigned as assistant Pastor of Our Lady of Lourdes Parish, Port Wentworth, Georgia. Also in 1952 he was made Chancellor of the Diocese of Savannah, and in 1956, Officialis of the Diocese of Savannah, and then appointed Papal Chamberlain, with the title of Very Reverend Monsignor.[32]

Bishop McDonald was in 1959 appointed Domestic Prelate, with the title of Right Reverend Monsignor and in 1963 appointed pastor of Blessed Sacrament Church, Savannah, Georgia. In 1967 he was appointed Vicar General for the Diocese of Savannah. On 4 July 1972, Pope Paul VI announced that he had been appointed as Bishop of Little Rock.[33]

Bishop McDonald was ordained a Bishop 5 September 1972 in the Cathedral of St. John the Baptist in Savannah, Georgia.[34]

On 7 September 1972, he was installed as Bishop of Little Rock at St. Andrew's Cathedral, Little Rock, Arkansas.

The Bishop of the Catholic Diocese of Little Rock, Bishop Andrew J. McDonald was installed in a two hour rite, making a moving plea for brotherhood and love.[35]

"There is only one sentiment which absorbs my heart today," he said, "this sentiment is so over whelming, it almost breaks my heart and soul. It is simple, but from the depths of my soul, and I mean it."[36]

"My priests, my religious, my sisters, my people, tall and short, thin and broad, black and white: of all denominations, of all walks of life in this beautiful state of Arkansas—I love you. I do already care about you. With God's help and the guidance of the Holy Spirit, I will live and if necessary, I will die to prove that I care; to prove that I love."[37]

His Excellency Bishop McDonald concluded with the same statement

The Most Reverend Albert Lewis Fletcher, D.D.

The Most Reverend Andrew J. McDonald, D.D.

with which he began his brief message:

"In the simplicity of my heart, I come to do Thy will, O God."[38]

The installation ceremony began at 11:00 a.m. with the sanctuary filled—visiting clergymen, including some 20 archbishops, bishops and abbots, led by the Knights of Columbus in their distinctive formal uniforms with crimson lined capes. Groups filed into the Cathedral to the music by Holy Trinity Seminary Choir of Dallas, accompanied by organ and trombone.[39]

The installing prelate and principle celebrant of the Mass was Archbishop Luigi Raimondi, the Apostolic Delegate to the United States. He was assisted by Archbishop Phillip M. Hannan of New Orleans. Other principal celebrants of the Mass were Bishop Lawrence Graves who was vicar general under Bishop Fletcher; Henry W. Miller, and Leonard Johnson, lectors and the Reverend Joseph Correnti.[40]

Chapter 18

Annunciation Academy, St. Joseph's School, Pine Bluff Catholic School and Convent Chapel

In the 1800's, there arose a building in the community to be devoted to the education of children under the system devised by the state.[1] The school was founded by Monsignor John M. Lucey and was situated on the same street and about six hundred feet west of St. Joseph's Church (first building).[2]

Bishop Edward Fitzgerald endorsed the purpose of the pastor, to invoke the Sisters of Charity of Nazareth, Kentucky to accept the opportunity to advance the interests of religion and Catholic Education in Pine Bluff. In September 1880, five sisters, with Sister Silvia O'Brien in charge, came to Pine Bluff. Sister Silvia remained in charge of the school for seven years.[3]

The first building (1880) was a "neat little cottage containing four rooms, with central hall, dining room and kitchen annex."[4] In 1881 the building was found to be inadequate, and the school purchased its present site and built a large two storied frame building which was (supposedly) to be sufficient for school and residential purposes. This building operated under capacity attendance.[5]

In May of 1901, the building was partially destroyed by fire, and restoration was completed, after which the building was removed to adjoining grounds, and on its former site was erected the present two storied brick building. This building was fully equipped with chapel, infirmary, library, laboratory, recitation and music rooms and stage.[6]

During the 1930's it became necessary to close the high school depart-

Annunciation Academy—circa 1903.

ment of Annunciation Academy, due to lack of funds during the depression years.[7] In the 1940's the school building was renovated,[8] and in 1954 four classrooms completed directly south of the old building and in 1966 in line with Diocesan regulations, a lay consultative school board was formed.[9] In 1967, The Sisters of Charity of Nazareth, Kentucky requested that St. Joseph's Church purchase for the Diocese of Little Rock, the Annunciation Academy property, following a trend that school properties be owned by the parish. Two appraisals were made, and it was decided to purchase this property from the Sisters for the sum of $160,000, which was the lowest of the two appraisals. His Excellency, Bishop Fletcher approved the transaction, and the transfer of the property to the diocese was effected 31 December 1967. The name of the school became St. Joseph's Catholic School.[10]

In order to provide larger classrooms and to relieve crowded conditions, it was decided to make some changes and to remodel the classrooms, by removing the Sisters dining room and kitchen to the second floor, and to eliminate the old stage—thus making the room much larger. The cafeteria was converted into a library, with the overall cost of the work approximately $30,000. The remodeled quarters were first used by students in 1968.[11]

During the years 1970–71, the school was staffed by the Sisters of Charity of Nazareth, and an increasing number of lay teachers, including Mrs. Harold Ward, Mrs. Gordon Seaton, Mrs. J. Edwin Karlovic, Mrs. Curtis

Students—Annunciation Academy—circa 1923. Front row, left to right, Ruby Brent, Emma Lehnert Barnes, Ruby Bishop, and May O'Keefe. Second row, left to right, Lucille Humrichouse, Laura Ferrara Failla, Rose Sylvester Haskins, Anna Roost Tillman, Juanita Brown, Caryl Colquitt Rucker, Philamena Sylvester. Standing, left to right, John Gordy and Jack Crutcher. Identification, courtesy of Mrs. W.A. Rucker and Miss Hilda Matz. Photograph, courtesy of Mr. John Webkes.

Rogers, Mrs. Delbert Bateman, Mr. Whatley T. Hill, Mrs. Harry King, Mrs. Charles LeSieur and Mrs. Rowland Barthet.[12]

On 27 April 1973, there appeared in The Guardian newspaper, the following:

"By Order of Bishop McDonald—Pine Bluff Catholic Schools To be Consolidated in the Fall"[13]

"For the 1973–74 academic year, the student bodies of St. Joseph's School, now predominantly white, and St. Peter's School, now predominantly black, will be merged." "Bishop Graves announced the consolidation in a Sunday pulpit letter last Sunday." "He said the consolidation had been decreed by His Excellency, Bishop Andrew J. McDonald." "One reason prompting the move, Bishop Graves said, was the need for extra space at St. Peter's School."[14]

"Additionally, the Auxiliary Bishop observed that, "it's obvious that the relationship between black and white is a problem of our whole nation, and this (consolidation) might possibly give some help to solve that problem in the future."[14]

Pine Bluff Catholic School held the 1973–74 school term, and closed in May 1974.[15]

The Convent Chapel

The Convent Chapel is located on the North side of the second floor of the old Annunciation Academy building. This chapel contains the five original stained-glass windows that were placed there when the Academy building was constructed in 1902.

This chapel was completely renovated during the tenure of Monsignor Gallagher, 1954–72; most probably about 1967. A plaque on the North wall states:

Daily we pray that "God Will Reward With Eternal Life All Those Who Have Done Us Good."

The James Batzos Family
The C. S. Conrod Family
The Albert Ernst Family
The Paul Finkbeiner Family
The Franey Family
The Steele Family
The Sylvestor Family
The Oleale Watts Family
The C.S.M.C. (Catholic Student Mission Crusade)
Helen Boyce
Dan Fratesi Family
Harry E. King Family
W. L. Rucker Family
John Rose Family
Primo Ruggeri Family
Sylvester Family
Mrs. John Self
K. of C. Council #1153
St. Joseph Church
Plaque's on the pews—West to East
Mary Ann and Paul Finkbeiner, Jr.
W. L. Rucker Family
St. Joseph Church
The Steele Family
Louis and Bass Aureli Family

Chapter 19

St. Joseph's Cemetery and Interments 1840–1913

St. Joseph's Parish Cemetery had its beginning on the 7th day of February 1874, the day Creed Taylor deeded part of the land that is now St. Joseph's Cemetery to the Church. Part of this land was a Catholic Cemetery several years before 1874, with earth raised burial lots and graded cemetery streets. Creed Taylor's letter of July 1873 to Monsignor John M. Lucey, Pastor of St. Joseph's Church, tells of the existing cemetery that had 17 known burials with grave markers. The oldest burial was in 1840. Creed Taylor did not know how many burials there were without grave markers or their dates. He also mentioned that this land (he deeded to the church) was part of an earlier Indian village.[1]

In his letter to Monsignor Lucey, Creed Taylor emphasized his concern about cemetery maintenance in future years, and wanted to avoid abandonment, as some cemeteries in Jefferson County had been abandoned. He admitted that he had relatives buried in the cemetery on his land and that was why he had purchased the land, so that he could hold it for a church cemetery.[2]

In 1944, our pastor (Monsignor Walshe) requested that a search of Jefferson County early land records be made of Section 31, Township 5 South, range 9 West. The search was an attempt to determine who owned the land previously, and the date when the earlier cemetery (before 1874) was started. The search proved negative. (The records may be in Arkansas County.) However, some of the Jefferson County records were as follows: United States to John Maulding 2 August 1838, 40 acres, certificate number 2824. The land changed ownership several times, and on 3 October 1852,

Solon B. Jones sold 27 acres to Creed Taylor for $100; and Creed Taylor sold 16 acres of this land, and retained the remaining 11 acres until 7 February 1874, the date he deeded the 11 acres to Bishop Fitzgerald.[3]

The historical interment records of St. Joseph's Cemetery reveal that a number of early prominent citizens who helped to build Pine Bluff and Jefferson County are buried in our cemetery. Among these are: James Scull, the first postmaster of Pine Bluff, William Carroll, a descendant of the Maryland Carroll family.[4] This family included Charles Carroll, the only Catholic signer of the Declaration of Independence, and John Carroll, first Bishop and Archbishop of the Primatial See of Baltimore, and Founder of Georgetown University 1789; Daniel Carroll, brother of John Carroll, member of the Continental Congress 1780–84, who signed the Articles of Confederation and served in the First Congress of the United States.[5]

St. Joseph's Cemetery is also the resting place of C. F. Moore, Civil Engineer who probably laid out the town site for Stuttgart, Arkansas, and Sarasen (1735–1832) the last of the Quapaw Indian chiefs in Arkansas.[6]

In Monsignor Lucey's cemetery records were found the following notes:

10 February 1876— Parish supper to raise money for a cemetery fence (181.95) was realized from this effort.

9 February 1877— Arch placed over cemetery entrance

27 May 1877— Bishop Fitzgerald dedicated St. Joseph's Cemetery

4 November 1887— Paid H. P. Bradford $4.00 for 4 loads of benches from church to cemetery and return.

5 November 1887— Monsignor Lucey read his first Mass in St. Joseph's Cemetery.

On 12 March 1902, Bishop Fitzgerald gave an easement or right of way to the city of Pine Bluff, a strip of cemetery land, 75 feet wide and 476 feet long, west of the bayou, to be used to open Pullen Street. This right of way was only used for street car tracks which required a high long trestle over Brump's Bayou. Pullen Street was open to all traffic in 1923. On 11 September 1950, cemetery land south of Pullen (not suitable for a cemetery) was sold, and the money added to St. Joseph's Cemetery Endowment Care Fund.[7]

By September of 1947, it became quite obvious that St. Joseph's Cemetery should expand, due to the growing number of Communicants in the parish. The following are excerpts from a letter written to Bishop Fletcher from Monsignor Walshe in 1947 concerning expansion of burial spaces for this parish.[8]

.... "Years ago when the present St. Joseph's Cemetery site was purchased, it was considered out of the city limits. The development of the city is now so, that our present cemetery is within the city limits. At present, there are not many vacant cemetery lots for sale, however, there will be many burials of families there, who own lots yet not occupied. On the other hand, there are ever so many people in my parish who do not own any cemetery space, and for whom I must eventually provide" . . . "it is my understanding that it would be impossible to buy land for cemetery purposes within the city limits. It would be almost impossible . . . . to go outside the city limits to secure land for a cemetery, because on all roads leading out of Pine Bluff in every direction (there) are situated suburban homes or cultivated farm lands, which property owners are not willing to give up" . . . "The City of Pine Bluff owns a very large tract of land . . . already laid out in lots for burial purposes. They are developing new sections and have offered the Church a reserved tract of land for a cemetery" . . . . "The City Council voted to set aside a particular section in Graceland Municipal Cemetery for exclusive use of Catholic burials" . . . .[9]

The offer made by the city met with the approval of Bishop Fletcher and an ordinance dated 1 March 1948, designated a portion of Edgewood Addition to Graceland Cemetery, as a Catholic burial ground.[10]

The following are interments in St. Joseph's Catholic Cemetery prior to 1913. This "cut-off" date (1913) was chosen because Arkansas birth and death records are on file at the Bureau of Vital Statistics in Little Rock, beginning in 1914. These interment records here recorded prior to the date Arkansas kept such records, may perhaps assist the genealogist or historian to locate a particular family in this area of our state.

From May 1874 to 11 November 1879 register kept by Thos. R. Hopkins. From 29 February 1880 register kept by Monsignor J. M. Lucey.

A

Abbene, Joseph— died 25 June 1907
Adams, James Eugene— died 18 December 1882
Annie Rebecca— died 10 April 1901
Antoine, Gabe— died 19 July 1880
Antoine, Paul— died 27 September 1884
Aureli, Dominick— died 28 July 1913

B

Babcock, Herbert— died 20 August 1886
Babcock, Mrs. Nora— died 19 May 1882
Boccarossa, Infant— died 5 December 1910
Barbler, Joseph— died 22 May 1889
Barbler, Mrs. Josie— died 13 July 1892
Barraque, Gustave— died 6 December 1887
Batterton, Infant— died 20 October 1892
Begley, Mrs. Fannie— died 18 October 1889
Begley, William J.— died 17 February 1884

Belluomini, G.— died 4 July 1886
Bennett, Mr.— died 28 June 1899
Berry, Mrs. D.— died 8 April 1906
Beunet, Ann Myrtle— died 12 May 1894
Bishop, Etta— died 24 October 1894
Bishop, Harry— died 18 September 1905
Bishop, Wilford Joseph— died 19 September 1910
Black, John Thomas— died 9 July 1896
Blackburn, James— died 4 July 1911
Blanchard, Charles— died 27 July 1897
Blanchard, Mrs. George— died 16 July 1889
Blaney, Mrs. Caroline— died 12 January 1898
Blaney, G. M.— died 26 April 1882
Boggins, Mary— died 16 November 1884
Bogy, Joseph (Dr.)— died 7 March 1880
Bolued, John— died 22 March 1882
Bond, Infant— died 7 November 1904
Bond, Josephine— died 17 July 1899
Bond, Mildred— died 29 March 1896
Boyce, Infant— died 14 September 1905
Boyce, Infant— died 17 December 1906
Boyce, Infant— died 17 May 1913
Boyce, Mrs. J. E.— died 27 May 1913
Bradley, John— died 15 February 1890
Brenke, Bernard S.— died 22 June 1907
Brenke, Infant— died 9 July 1910
Brennan, James— died 8 September 1893
Brennan, Mamie— died 24 November 1897
Brennan, Mrs. Sarah— died 2 July 1909
Brown, Annie Jewel— died 3 September 1902
Brown, Mrs.— died 30 June 1893
Buck, Infant— died 27 July 1889
Buck, Mrs. Thomas E.— died 13 April 1885
Buckingham, Mrs. Nora— died 7 March 1890
Bullard, Emma Mary— died 18 September 1887
Bullard, John— died 2 August 1886
Burdick, Infant— died 6 November 1899
Burgan, Thomas— died 1880

C

Cady, Bridget Wright— died 15 November 1874
Cady, John— died 8 November 1889
Cady, John Andrew— died 27 September 1888
Cady, John Francis— died 19 October 1900
Calhoun, E. H.— died 15 November 1899
Calhoun, Eva May— died 5 August 1888
Calhoun, Lizzie Maria— died 13 February 1893
Campbell, James— died 23 November 1890
Carroll, David Williamson— died 4 January 1883
Carroll, William— died 4 May 1885

Carver, Mrs. Leonard—died 29 July 1912
Cartwright, Mrs.—died 14 March 1900
Cartwright, Mrs. Belle—died 2 October 1904
Cartwright, G. E.—died 17 March 1900
Cerder (?), Tim—died 29 October 1897
Chalhenpe (?), Mrs. Catherine—died 29 September 1901
Charlan (?), Margaret—died 20 November 1908
Chestnut, Charles—died 30 August 1890
Chestnut, John Francis—died 4 December 1885
Childress, Infant—died 16 June 1899
Childress, Marie—died 18 February 1913
Childress, Thelma—died 19 April 1910
Childress, Thomas B.—died 30 December 1907
Childress, Williamette—died 6 December 1886
Childress, W. J. (Dr.)—died 28 March 1894
Chilson, Infant—22 March 1904
Clague, Infant—20 August 1888
Clay, Mrs. Elizabeth—5 August 1895
Claxton, Virgil—died 5 April 1906
Cling, Mrs. Angelina—died 5 September 1904
Cobb, Fanny—died 10 November 1885
Collet, Estelle—died 10 June 1886
Collins, Mabel—died 21 February 1906
Collins, Tim—died 23 December 1891
Comstock, Julia—died 15 March 1913
Condon, Infant—died 8 May 1887
Conesso, Joseph—died 19 August 1895
Conly, Idelia—died 30 September 1877
Conyers, Walter G.—died 21 April 1904
Cook, Mrs. Charles—died 16 August 1911
Cook, Lawrence—died 18 August 1889
Corder, Mrs. A. P.—died 10 June 1908
Corder, Mrs. Tim—died 22 June 1895
Cosotte, Mrs. John—died 10 September 1898
Costello, John—died 5 October 1903
Cox, Mrs.—died 23 August 1888

D

Daley, Jerry—died 25 January 1878
Daroux, Alma Emma Louise—died 19 December 1892
Davis, Mrs. Caroline—died 20 September 1889
Davis, George—died 23 August 1900
Delaney, James—died 3 August 1874
Delaney, Mary—died 4 October 1881
Dellman, J. H.—died 7 February 1903
Dellman, Mrs. J. H. Sr. and child reinterred 5 May 1903
Dellman, Margaret—died 22 February 1911
Dennison, Albert—died 20 August 1899
Denny, Thomas—died 21 December 1897
Derriseaux, J. B.—died 16 March 1895

Derriseux, Mrs. Mary—died 18 January 1913
Dieticta (?), J. C.—died 25 September 1900
Dietz, Joseph—died 24 May 1900
Dodge, Charles Earl—died 21 September 1886
Dodge, Pearl, died 6 July 1887
Doherty, Infant—died 11 December 1891
Donovan, Allien Eliza—died 9 April 1903
Donovan, Mrs. Eliza—died 23 October 1898
Donovan, Infant—died 3 May 1900
Donovan, Infant—died 2 October 1904
Donovan, Infant—died 20 February 1906
Donovan, John—died 23 September 1885
Donovan, Mrs. John—died 2 October 1904
Donovan, Malachi—died 20 December 1895
Donovan, Mrs. Malachi—died 3 January 1901
Doroux, Mrs. E.—died 24 November 1898
Dowd, James—died 9 August 1886
Doyle, Annie—died 11 November 1879
Doyle, Annie—died 19 October 1889
Doyle, Bridget—died 29 October 1879
Doyle, Dennis—died 15 January 1884
Doyle, John—died 7 November 1876
Doyle, Joseph Thomas—died 29 October 1879
Doyle, Patrick—died 13 August 1876
Duelmer, Clara Regina—died 7 September 1896
Dugan, Arthur—died 28 April 1883
Dugan, John—died 3 April 1913
Duggan, Infant (twin)—died 27 July 1904
Duggan, Infant (twin)—died 27 July 1904
Duggan, Stephen—died 11 December 1905
Dulmer, Nellie—died 16 September 1897
Durner, Andrew—died 22 August 1893
Durner, Bessie—died 17 October 1897
Dutlinger, John—died 21 October 1887
Dutlinger, William—died 22 August 1881
Dwyer, Mr.—died 8 December 1912

E

Egan, Florence Agnes—died 19 November 1892
Egan, William—died 21 October 1891
Eheard, Infant—died 10 September 1888
Elias, Habib—died 4 May 1908
Embry, Infant—died 1 November 1891
Embry, Nellie—died 11 June 1886

F

Fannin, Michael—died 20 May 1912
Faro, Joe—died 3 May 1895

Fay, Martin—died 6 June 1883
Feeny, John—died 26 September 1888
Fenwick, J. E.—died 24 March 1896
Ferguson, Zachary Howard—died 26 March 1908
Ferguson, Z. T.—died 1 July 1894
Fereis, Ed—died 14 April 1878
Fiest, Joseph—died 22 July 1884
Finta, Mrs. Anna—died 28 February 1909
Fitzpatrick, Bernard—died May 1874
Fitzjohn, Infant—died 11 November 1886
Flourney, Chester—died 8 January 1889
Flynn, Charles Henry—died 4 August 1902
Flynn, Margurite—died 4 August 1902
Flynn, Mollie—died 23 October 1889
Flynn, Mrs. Obe—died 26 June 1888
Foley, Michael—died 14 November 1910
Ford, Margaret—died 2 September 1886
Forrester, Patrick—died 23 July 1887
Foti, Catherine—died 18 May 1909
Foti, Carmela—died 20 March 1901
Foti, Mrs. Carmela—died 25 March 1899
Foti, Frank—died 7 August 1905
Foti, Infant—died 5 September 1896
Foti, John—died 13 October 1905
Foti, Vicuizo—died 1 November 1904
Fox, J. C.—died 17 March 1907
Fox, Mrs. J. C.—died 29 June 1905
Francis, Mrs. P. J.—died 12 April 1908
Franey, Elizabeth Mable—died 6 June 1888
Franey, Mrs. James—died 17 September 1892
Franey, J. F.—died 24 November 1897
Frawley, Patrick—died 22 August 1895
Friel, D. H.—died 8 November 1903

G

Gallagher, Michael—died 22 September 1888
Gallagher, Patrick—died 20 August 1891
Galvin, Michael—died 6 December 1886
Galvin, Patrick—died 27 August 1885
Garretty, Thos.,—died 28 December 1875
Geary, Mrs.—died 12 September 1899
Genevay, Albert—died 31 December 1903
Genevay, Eugene—died 8 September 1892
Genevay, Mrs. Kate—died 20 February 1908
Gill, Mrs. Elizabeth—died 17 February 1907
Gill, Infant—died 13 November 1905
Gill, Nathan—died 28 August 1895
Gill, Rube—died 22 March 1903
Gilman, Mr.—died 23 February 1891
Gilman, Mrs. E. J.—died 22 May 1898

Glogner, Harry Ed—died 8 June 1911
Gossett, Peter—died 7 April 1891
Grady, Mrs. Peter—died 26 October 1888
Grady, Peter T.—died 29 June 1889
Green, Annie—died 22 June 1895
Green, Thomas—died 8 September 1899
Greenwood, Mrs. Margaret J.—died 27 June 1898
Greer, Lottie Ellen—died 22 August 1896
Grescheck, Mrs.—died 13 October 1894
Griffin, Mrs.—died 3 January 1886
Griffin, Thomas—died May 1880
Guynn, Robert Lee—died 9 January 1913

H

Hackett, Mrs. Eliza—died 18 July 1884
Haley, John—died 21 December 1883
Hall, Mrs. L. A.—died 1 February 1902
Halpin, Edward—died 15 May 1884
Halpin, Mrs.—died 9 March 1888
Hamilton, Henrietta—died 6 August 1866
Hamilton, Henry—died 16 February 1859
Hamilton, Dr. J. T.—died 9 September 1888
Hamilton, Leonore—died 14 February 1852
Hamilton, Mary Eliza—no date
Hamilton, Manett Feliciana—died 6 May 1868
Hamilton, Robert Emmett—no date
Hanley, Mr.—died 6 February 1910
Hanly, Michael—died 17 September 1883
Hartnet, Annie—died 4 June 1882
Hartnet, Infant—died 20 September 1893
Havis, Mrs. Ferdinand—died 13 August 1886
Hawkins, Joseph B.—died 11 May 1894
Helm, Infant—died 1 July 1905
Hemsteager, Joseph Aloysius—died 20 December 1890
Hemsteager, William Joseph—died 4 April 1889
Henberry, _____—died 1897
Henderson, Julia Leone—died 1 August 1887
Hepburn, Barney F.—died 16 April 1885
Hessig, Frank—died 6 March 1887
Higdon, J. E.—died 5 November 1904
Higgins, Mrs. Susanna—died 31 mo. (?) 1884
Hilton, Thomas H.—died 9 July 1897
Holden, Annie—died 18 June 1890
Holland, Mrs. Annie Wolf—died 17 January 1904
Holland, James Sell—died 22 July 1901
Holland, John Leonard—died 29 October 1900
Hope, John Herbert—died 17 September 1891
Hope, Raymond—died 12 July 1894
Hopkins, Catherine Ellen—died 20 September 1874
Hopkins, George Henry—died 21 December 1899

127

Howard, Ed—died 24 August 1875
Howard, James—died 27 March 1894
Howard, John—died 24 August 1875
Howe, Infant—died 12 December 1913
Huggard, John—died 8 September 1894
Huggard, Richard—died 25 September 1886
Hughes, Edward—died 5 February 1886
Hughes, John—died 9 June 1900
Hulsiz, James—died 2 December 1885
Hume, Mrs. B. H.—died 23 June 1906

I

Imbrey, Joseph—died 7 September 1888
Imbrey, Mary—died 2 September 1888

J

Jackson, John—died 4 July 1911
Jones, Mrs. Bob—died 8 December 1902
Jones, George Joseph—died 28 November 1897
Jones, Infant—died 24 December 1905
Jones, Richard B.—died 27 December 1906
Jones, Robert—died 24 February 1899
Johnson, Alla M.—died 27 September 1909
Johnson, Infant—died 11 February 1913
Johnson, John W.—died 31 March 1902
Johnson, Mrs. Lou—died 29 March 1907
Johnson, William—died 30 January 1906
Joyce, Martin—died 19 February 1880
Juarez, Felipe—died 15 October 1902

K

Kalkbrenner, Henry—died 25 August 1904
Kane, Michael—died 26 May 1884
Kavriz, Mrs.—died 4 June 1911
Kelly, Birdie—died 21 May 1887
Kelly, Daniel—died 31 January 1877
Kelly, Mrs. Mary—died 28 October 1890
Kelly, Myrtle—died 23 May 1887
Kembramer, Frank Thomas—died 19 August 1900
Kenna, Thomas—died 5 November 1883
Kerwin, Catherine—died 25 October 1884
Kerwin, Dan, Sr.—died 22 October 1894
Kerwin, Daniel—died 8 October 1909
Kerwin, Daniel—died 26 October 1899 (reinterred in another lot)
Kilday, Martin—died 26 January 1878
Kilray, Anna Emma—died 9 July 1892
King, Infant—died 4 November 1907

Kinney, John—died 11 January 1885
Kramer, Paul—died 14 March 1893

L

Lacardi, Infant—died 25 November 1893
Lacardi, Infant—died 22 May 1899
Larcardi, Minnie—died 8 March 1896
Lampert, Infant—died 20 April 1902
Lampert, John Edward—died 10 July 1903
Lampert, Lennie—died 15 October 1898
Laude, Joseph—died 28 July 1906
Lauders, Mrs. Amanda—died 8 January 1907
Lehman, Alford—died 16 April 1896
Lehman, George—died 2 November 1900
Lehnert, John—died 31 December 1903
Leidinger, Louis—died 8 July 1896
Leland, Annie (or Ida)—died 3 August 1890
Lemmans, Mrs. Ellen—died 11 August 1886
Leonard, Balf (?)—died 23 April 1886
Leonard, John Edmund—died 8 August 1888
Leonard, John J.—died 24 June 1885
Lihoff (?), J.—died 2 December 1912
Lindsey, John Andrew—died 28 September 1888
Lomonico, Mary—died 26 December 1898
Loring, Ellar—died 9 March 1911
Lovelady, Maude—died 4 February 1908
Lubry, Infant—died 31 May 1894
Lubry, Infant—died 15 October 1898
Lucke, _____—died 13 October 1910
Lucke, A. B.—died 6 August 1906
Lynch, Owen—died 25 October 1883
Lynch, Patrick—died 8 July 1907
Lynch, Patrick—died 31 October 1907

Mc

McBride, Bernard C.—died 16 March 1888
McCarthy, John—died 5 January 1894
McConnell, Infant—died 9 July 1913
McCormick, John—died 30 April 1881
McCrane, John—died 24 November 1888
McDermott, John C.—died 24 September 1901
McDermott, Mrs. John C.—died 25 September 1900
McEvoy, John—died 9 October 1894
McGhee, Michael—died 10 June 1908
McGinnis, _____—died 21 January 1903
McGlynn, Annie—died 3 July 1881
McGlynn, Annie—died 10 July 1882
McGlynn, Catherine—died 13 August 1879

McGlynn, Mrs. Catherine—died 10 January 1890
McGlynn, Infant—died 10 August 1879
McGlynn, James—died 13 July 1881
McGlynn, Katie—died 1887
McGlynn, Mary Ann—died 19 August 1879
McGlynn, Mary Ann—died 1885
McGlynn, Mathew—died 19 October 1876
McGlynn, Mattie—died 1884
McGlynn, Patrick—died 26 November 1889
McGlynn, Peter—died 12 July 1903
McGregor, Andrew—died 1 December 1888
McKevit, John P.—died 9 May 1893
McKnight, Allie May—died 20 November 1904
McKnight, James—died 3 January 1893
McMahon, John—died 17 May 1889
McManus, Infant—died 31 March 1907
McNally, Adele Carroll—reinterred St. Joseph's Cemetery summer 1892—date of death unknown
McNally, Charles—died 7 January 1904
McNally, (John?)—died 1885
McNally, John—reinterred St. Joseph's Cemetery summer 1892—date of death unknown
McNally, Mary—died 10 October 1896
McNulty, Thomas—died 18 December 1904
McQueeny, William—died 10 September 1877

M

Maguire, Thomas—died 1880
Maher, Mrs. Johanna—died 20 February 1908
Mahar, John T.—died 5 October 1900
Mahar, William—died 4 December 1902
Malfitti, Lorenzo—died 3 January 1886
Malley, D. P.—died 19 December 1906
Malley, Infant—died 25 October 1877
Malley, Infant—died 6 June 1908
Malley, Mary Frances—died 16 December 1876
Malone, Thomas—died 16 December 1888
Maney, Mrs.—died 25 December 1913
Manley, Patrick—died 11 February 1901
Many, Martin—died 18 October 1881
Mason, Ellen—died 23 October 1881
Massanelli, Infant—died 28 December 1912
Matz, Barbara Josephine—died 13 August 1909
Mayer, Ida—died 28 March 1912
Meyer, John—died 21 October 1877
Meyer, William—died 13 December 1881
Michellotte, Lawrence—died 12 September 1897
Miller, John—died 13 December 1884
Mitchell, John—died 8 December 1881
Montgomery, Robert Alexander—died 27 May 1886

Moore, Thomas—died 14 September 1888
Mora, Michael—died 26 November 1896
Moran, William—died 27 August 1877
Morrow, Morris—died 31 December 1908
Moser, Frank Adam—died 18 October 1891
Moser, Joseph Charles—died 7 June 1895
Mountain, Mrs. Sarah Roundtree—died 12 April 1889
Mulligan, Thomas—died 6 June 1899
Murphy, Catherine Beatrice—died 2 November 1877
Murphy, Frances—died August 1878
Murphy, John—died 23 August 1877
Murphy, John P.—died 16 December 1892
Murphy, Patrick—died 5 November 1890
Murphy, Robert Ernest Lee—died 23 March 1884
Murphy, Solon Washington—died 27 December 1881
Murr, Max—died 27 June 1878
Murray, Charles—died 23 November 1885
Murray, James—died 25 November 1889
Murray, Mrs. Peter—died 4 February 1898
Murtaugh, John—died 3 October 1885
Mustachia, Maggie Laurine—died 5 February 1899
Mustachia, Mary Lena—died 16 April 1891
Mustachia, Paschal—died 1 November 1910

O

Oaks, Infant—died 30 July 1905
Oaks, J. H.—died 26 April 1905
Oaks, Ruby—died 15 July 1902
O'Brian, James D.—died 8 November 1895
O'Brian, Johanna—died 5 January 1911
O'Connell, Emily—died 25 October 1883
O'Connell, Emma May—died 1 November 1886
O'Donnell, Peter—died 5 September 1875
O'Keiff, Anthony—died 30 June 1905
O'Keiff, Mrs. B.—died 6 July 1909
O'Keiff, James Charles Joseph—died 13 November 1897
O'Leary, Dennis—died 3 January 1883
O'Leary, John—died 17 November 1890
O'Leary, Odellia—died 23 March 1890
Olson, Eli—died 11 January 1911
Olson, Mrs. John—died 7 March 1909
O'Mark (?), Infant (twin)—died 2 January 1898
O'Mark (?), Infant (twin)—died 2 January 1898
Omcirck, Edwin—died 29 May 1900
Omcirck, Infant (twin)—reinterred (?) 23 June 1900
Omcirck, Infant (twin)—reinterred (?) 23 June 1900
Omcirck, Infant—died 8 January 1904
Omcirck, Joseph—died 9 May 1894
O'Neil, Frank Joseph—died 2 August 1900
O'Neil, Maggie—died 27 September 1883

O'Rourke, Mrs.—died 3 May 1899
O'Rourke, William—died 8 July 1907
O'Sullivan, Florence—died 18 February 1899
O'Sullivan, Florence (Jr.)—died 13 September 1876
O'Sullivan, Mary Ellen—died 26 April 1877
O'Sullivan, Mrs. Mary Florence—died 14 February 1899
Ormond, Mrs. Annie—died 31 July 1888
Ormond, John—died 14 June 1892
Ormond, John George—died 16 September 1888
Ormond, Thomas—died 2 August 1888

P

Palmer, Tom—died 23 June 1899
Palmer, Willie—died 18 June 1894
Parenti, Infant—died 18 March 1908
Patterson, Mrs. E. M.—died 4 December 1911
Pendleton, P. H., Dr.—died 26 March 1899
Perry, Jack—died 3 February 1904
Perry, Mrs. Jack—died 4 February 1901
Philpot, Mrs. C. E.—died 8 November 1907
Pichi, Infant—died 3 March 1912
Pickett, George—died 30 April 1901
Picket, Infant—died 28 October 1898
Poff, Oscar Thomas—died 18 November 1882
Pordini, Domenico—died 12 October 1894
Portis, Charles B., Rev.—died December 1893
Portis, James—died 4 July 1900
Portis, John—died 10 August 1899
Primeau, Mrs.—died 26 May 1899
Prye, Mary E.—died 10 June 1903

R

Rawls, Mrs. Rosa—died 4 August 1898
Redding, Infant—died 4 June 1901
Redmann, Adeline—died 22 February 1877
Redmand, Infant—died 7 November 1904
Reidenger, Louis C.—died 18 November 1911
Reynolds, G. G.—died 27 November 1875
Reynolds, John—died 8 December 1893
Reynolds, Katie—died 14 December 1893
Rider, Mrs. Anna—died 15 October 1909
Rocher, Marie—died 20 August 1895
Rodgers, Infant—died 12 May 1906
Roney, John—died 20 January 1885
Rooney, Thomas—died 18 December 1888
Rose, Joseph—died 20 October 1900
Ross, Mary—died December 1906
Rosser, Eli—died 11 January 1911

Rudder, Mrs. Mary—died 27 August 1886
Ruggeri, Augusto—died 1909
Ryan, James—died 3 July 1881

S

Saconi, Eddie C.—died 28 June 1894
Saconi, Joseph—died 9 March 1890
Sacconi, Mrs.—died 20 August 1907
Saracen, Chief of the Quapaws—reinterred 21 January 1905
Satterwhite, Mrs.—died 9 December 1912
Savary, D.—died 3 March 1899
Schaep, George John Peter—died 19 June 1888
Schlater, Infant—died 16 June 1900
Schnable, Annie—died 20 February 1909
Schneider, Mrs. Nannie—died 15 May 1903
Scott, D. E.—died 22 August 1900
Scull, Frances—died 3 November 1911
Scull, Hewes—died 27 September 1881
Scull, James Hewes—died 13 September 1899
Scull, Mrs. J. H.—died 6 December 1886
Scull, James Knox—no date
Scull, Mrs. Louisiana Philipena—died 16 September 1909
Scull, Mary—moved October 1899 from Bellwood
Scull, Mary—died 5 June 1885
Scull, Nicholas—moved October 1899 from Bellwood
Scull, Roberta A.—died 16 February 1875
Scull, William Frederick—died 25 November 1874
Shim, Prudentiana—died 19 September 1885
Shinall, Mrs. Charles—died 9 April 1899
Shinall, Infant—died 16 April 1896
Simpson, Maggie—died 22 August 1898
Simpson, William—died 15 July 1898
Sister Angela (of Sisters of Charity of Nazareth)—died 19 January 1887
Sister Clarissa—died 14 November 1911
Sister Eudosia—died 5 August 1881
Sister Mary Sebastian—died 23 October 1906
Sister Placida—died 28 February 1906
Smidt, Charles—died 12 August 1899
Smith, Mrs. C. D.—died 29 July 1908
Smith, Joseph William—died 10 June 1885
Smith, Joseph Willian—died 25 June 1895
Smith, Silas Joseph—died 11 May 1904
Stahl, Jacob—died 20 September 1882
Stahl, Joseph—died 19 October 1882
Steele, Joseph Aloyisuis—died 25 June 1894
Steele, W. C.—died 5 March 1912
Strager, Mrs. H. C.—died 31 May 1895
Striver, Barbara—died 26 January 1884
Stroble, Infant—died 5 August 1901
Stroble, Joseph—died 28 June 1904

Stroble, Maggnie—died 22 September 1904
Sullivan, C. J.—died 16 October 1894
Sullivan, Eugene—died 1 August 1885
Swift, John—died 1880
Sylvester, Antonio—died 27 October 1892
Sylvester, Mrs. Charles—died 16 May 1913
Sysmanszek, Annie—died 8 May 1892

T

Taggart, Augusta Cecilia—died 30 May 1900
Taggart, Fred—died 12 April 1891
Taggart, Zelma Marie—died 14 June 1894
Tague, Mrs. Mary—died 23 May 1905
Taylor, Lucille—died 12 December 1909
Teague, Frank J.—died 8 October 1907
Teems, (?) Mrs. Mary—died 12 September 1893
Terry, Henry Clay—died 8 February 1891
Terry, Infant—died 5 January 1888
Terry, Infant—died 22 February 1890
Theilin, Mamie—died 7 June 1890
Thompson, Clarence—died 20 September 1876
Thompson, James—died 2 July 1895
Thornhill, Mrs. C. E.—died 1 September 1911
Tierney, Frances—died 9 July 1886
Tierney, John—died 24 September 1895
Tierney, Mrs. John—died 31 July 1890
Tierney, Joseph James—died 28 August 1895
Tierney, Peter M.—died 3 October 1911
Timmons, William—died 17 November 1876
Tomaszewski, John N.—died 5 July 1906
Truehart, Edward—died 21 August 1888
Truseak, J. E. or Truehart—died 1885
Treutel, Infant—died 25 July 1893
Treutel, Infant—died 2 August 1898
Tuomy, Joseph—died 28 October 1885
Turney, Infant—died 2 July 1874

U

Ulte, Martin—died 27 March 1909
Unnamed, Infant—died 28 September 1909

V

Vandeventer, Joseph—died 20 October 1902
Vaughan, Grant—died 22 July 1896
Vaughan, Samuel—died 15 May 1891
Vaugine, Caroline—died September 1898
Vechia, Mary—died 13 September 1909
Verret, Edwin—died 12 January 1902

Verret, Infant—died 13 December 1888
Verret, J. T.—died 25 September 1889
Verret, Lucille—died 20 September 1900
Verret, Orvil—died 20 May 1897
Vowell, Frank—died 19 May 1905

W

Walker, Eulalia—died 22 June 1889
Walker, James N.—died 19 January 1887
Walker, J. M. C.—died 21 August 1840
Walker, John M.—died 23 August 1893
Walker, Joseph W.—died 4 January 1903
Walker, Mrs. Nora—died 3 July 1913
Walker, Robert Woods—died 27 January 1842
Walter, John—died 21 October 1906
Waskoski, Agnes—died 24 December 1905
Waskoski, Ermine—died 18 July 1907
Waskoski, Henry—died 5 December 1896
Waskoski, Infant—died 29 October 1909
Waskoski, Peter—died 20 February 1906
Watts, John R.—died 27 February 1913
Weaver, Frank—died 27 October 1894
Weaver, Katherine—died 9 October 1899
Weaver, Lena—died 9 January 1899
Weaver, Ralph Joseph—died 10 September 1899
Weaver, Thomas G.—died 6 October 1892
Webkes, Infant—died 11 October 1910
Welsh, Patrick—died 13 June 1875
Werling, Willie—died 28 May 1895
Werner, Charles—died 14 July 1883
West, Infant—died 28 August 1893
White, Thomas—died 23 January 1888
Whitworth, Mrs. Plunetta—died 15 August 1898
Willerman, Mrs. Louise—died 27 September 1903
Williams, C. F.—died 30 March 1899
Williams, John B.—died 23 November 1907
Williams, Joseph—died 13 June 1905
Winter, Mrs. Mary—died 13 March 1897
Wise, Mrs. G. W.—died 14 June 1889
Wise, Infant—died September 1889
Wolf, Mrs. Ethel—died 14 March 1913
Wood, Mrs. Guy—died 9 May 1904
Woolford, Infant—died 18 March 1888
Wright, Pauline—died 18 December 1893

Chapter 20

Laymen of St. Joseph's

It would be impossible to list all of the outstanding laymen of St. Joseph's who have contributed their talents so willingly through the years. The following ladies and gentlemen are only a few of the many communicants who have helped this parish grow throughout the years.

Mr. John B. Brenke, son of the late Mr. & Mrs. Frank Brenke was born in Effingham, Illinois about 1887 and moved to Pine Bluff in 1903, working as a machinist for the Cotton Belt Railroad until 1922. He worked for the Pine Bluff Iron Works from 1922 through 1942, and then returned to the railroad until his retirement in 1958. Mr. Brenke was a charter member of the Knights of Columbus Council 1153, and St. Joseph's Altar Society. He died, Pine Bluff, Arkansas 4 June 1979.[1]

Mr. Albert Charles Ernst, Sr., son of the late Annie Bell and Louis Gottlieb Ernst was born about 1901, a native of New Orleans, Louisiana. He was reared and educated in New Orleans, and began his career with the railroads in 1915 when he started working for the Illinois Central Railroad as a stock clerk in Pine Bluff. He served as district storekeeper, stock clerk from 1923–1941; traveling storekeeper, assistant general storekeeper in 1952. He was made assistant purchasing agent and general storekeeper in 1960 and retired in 1965 and in 1966 was employed by T and N Electric Company of Pine Bluff as purchasing agent.[2]

Mr. Ernst served St. Joseph's Church for 50 years as accountant. He served on the Parish Council in a number of positions and on the St. Joseph's School Board. He was a member of the Pine Bluff Council 1153 of the Knights of Columbus and served as Grand Knight for five consecutive terms. He also served as state deputy for the Knights of Columbus for four years, was elected to the office of Faithful Navigator for the Pine Bluff

Assembly of the Fourth Degree Knights of Columbus, and made an honorary life member of the Knights in 1973.[3]

Mr. Ernst was presented a papal medal, "Oro Ecclesia Et Pontifice" by Bishop Andrew J. McDonald in March of 1976. Mr. Ernst died in Pine Bluff, 20 April 1976.[4]

Mr. J. Frank Franey was born about 1886 and was a retired communications officer at the Pine Bluff Arsenal. He was a native of Pine Bluff and attended Pine Bluff schools. He served two terms as Grand Knight of the Knights of Columbus, and was a member of the Pine Bluff Rotary Club and United Commercial Travelers.

Mr. Franey died 21 September 1969 in Pine Bluff.[5]

Mrs. B. A. Holcombe moved to Pine Bluff in 1868 from Union County, Arkansas. She was an active participant in the early affairs of St. Joseph's parish, serving as vice-president in charge of a bazaar to make improvements to the church property when Father Duggan served St. Joseph's,— 1871. Mrs. Holcombe died in Pine Bluff 10 December 1927.[6]

Mr. Leslie E. Leas, son of the late Augusta Fischer and Russell D. Leas was born in 1896. He served as an officer in the Army during World War II. He was a retired employee of Arkansas Power and Light Company where he served as assistant secretary and later secretary-treasurer of the Company.

Mr. Leas served faithfully for many years as secretary of the Board of Wardens at St. Joseph's Church. He was a member of the Jefferson County Equalization Board, the Arkansas-Missouri Association of Tax Representatives and the Pine Bluff Parks Commission. He was a member of the boards of the Jefferson County Department of Public Welfare, Jefferson County Tuberculosis Association, and the Arkansas Society for Crippled Children. He was a charter member of the Jefferson County-Pine Bluff Kiwanis Club and a Fourth Degree member of the Knights of Columbus.

Mr. Leas died in Pine Bluff, 26 August 1981.[7]

Mrs. Louisiana Philipena Scull was born 12 December 1819 at Arkansas Post and at her death, the Pine Bluff Graphic reported that she was Pine Bluff's oldest resident. She married in 1837, Mr. Hewes Scull, a cousin. Mrs. Scull was quite active in the early days of St. Joseph's Church, and the Pine Bluff Graphic stated that she had been a nurse during the Civil War, and had lived in Pine Bluff for 64 years.

Mrs. Scull died in Pine Bluff, 14 September 1909.[8]

Chapter 21

St. Peter's Mission

During some years previous to 1887, The Right Reverend Monsignor John M. Lucey did pioneer work in Pine Bluff, by purchasing a block of ground on which he erected a brick building known as the Colored Industrial Institute. In 1887–1888, the black population of Jefferson County was about 48,000 people, and at that time, Pine Bluff itself had about 6,000 black people.[1]

In 1889, the building was finished and school began with an enrollment of 143 pupils, in charge of four Sisters of Charity of Nazareth as teachers. The school was under the direction of a board of seven directors: J. M. Bocage, Mayor of the city; J. W. Owens, Judge of the County; the Right Reverend Monsignor John M. Lucey, pastor of St. Joseph's Church; Ferdinand Havis; Wiley Jones; W. P. Grace and J. M. Gracie.[2]

Special courses in the domestic arts and home economics were given for the women, with mechanical studies and farming for the men.[3]

In 1894, Monsignor Lucey built the first St. Peter's Church.[4] This first church was erected through the (efforts) of the editors and readers of a Boston, Massachusetts newspaper, "The Pilot," who contributed donations for that purpose.[5]

Monsignor Lucey saw the necessity of a resident priest at St. Peter's mission, and to that end he secured the Reverend Patrick J. Sheehy in 1894–95,[6] whose sole duty was to administer to the spiritual needs of the black people.[7] Father Sheehy lived in a little room back of the church, since as yet there was no priest's house.[8]

Thus with a resident pastor, St. Peter's was no longer a mission church of St. Joseph's, and when Father Sheehy closed his labors in Pine Bluff, his work was taken up by the Josephite Fathers.[9]

In 1897, St. Peter's Academy opened, and in 1903, the present church building was erected, designed by T. C. Windham, a black architect, and was used on All Saints Day 1903 for the first time.[10]

Chapter 22

Blessed Sacrament, Grady and Cemetery Records

St. Paul's, Noble Lake and St. Patrick's, Sulphur Springs

Blessed Sacrament Church at Grady is a mission church of St. Joseph's. There have been four church buildings at Grady. The first one was built prior to 1894, and was destroyed by a cyclone in 1897. The second church was dedicated in 1905, the third church dedicated in 1914, and the present building built in 1965.[1]

Blessed Sacrament Church has a cemetery adjacent to it, with the following interments prior to 1900.

D

Dennis, Mary E.—third daughter of J. C. and Elizabeth Wood, born 3 September 1858, died 23 June 1897

H

Hall, Eliza F.—second wife of John I. Hall, born 5 February 1849, died 28 August 1885

Hall, Infant—daughter of J. W. and Leonora Hall, birth and death 28 January 1888

Hall, James W.—husband of Leonora J. Hall, born 25 January 1861, died 16 February 1887

Hall, Leonora J.—wife of James W. Hall, born 6 January 1868, died 9 February 1887

Cemetery, Blessed Sacrament Church, Grady, Arkansas.

Hall, Mattie E.—third wife of John I. Hall, born 16 October 1853, died 15 February 1887

Hall, Walter F.—son of J. I. and E. F. Hall, born 18 August 1883, died 14 December 1883

Hall, Willie E.— daughter of J. W. and Leonora Hall, born 9 July 1884, died 31 January 1887

Hardin, Ethel—born 1895, died 1899

Hardin, Infant—son of Bertie and Jeff Hardin, died 1892

Hardin, Maggie—daughter of Thomas and Eliza Hardin, born 6 June 1871, died 8 June 1899

K

Kelly, Dennis—born 22 October 1856, died 5 February 1893

R

Richmond, Bertha—daughter of C. N. and J. A. Richmond, born 10 December 1883, died 1 December 1886

Richmond, Charles H.—son of C. N. and N. S. Richmond, born 9 March 1903, died 21 March 1903

Richmond, Corine—daughter of C. N. and J. A. Richmond, born 19 January 1887, died 11 February 1887

W

Wood, Eleanorae—wife of Fred A. Wood, born in Jefferson County 21 October 1845, died in Grady, Arkansas 9 May 1885

Wood, Elizabeth—wife of Jesse C. Wood, born in Hopkinsville, Kentucky 30 January 1818, died 13 November 1876 in Grady, Arkansas

Wood, Emma—"Little Emma" born 14 February 1884, died 17 February 1884

Wood, Infant—son of Fred A. and E. E. Wood, birth and death 25 April 1885

Wood, Mary—"Little Mary" daughter of Fred A. and E. E. Wood, born 21 December 1878, died 23 December 1878

Wood, Sarah C.—daughter of Jesse C. and Elizabeth Wood, born in Jefferson County 12 December 1860, died 22 September 1877

Wood, W. H.—born 23 March 1851, died 13 March 1891

St. Paul's Church, Noble Lake, Arkansas

On 2 February 1852, Emma Kelley for the consideration of $5.00 deeded to Andrew Byrne, Bishop of Little Rock, Arkansas, land situated on the South ½ of South West ½ of South West fractional quarter of fractional section 30, Township 6, South of Range 7 West, lying on Westside of Noble Lake, Jefferson County, Arkansas (about 2 acres). It is the author's understanding that a church, St. Paul's was built on this site at one time, but later dismantled.[2] It is believed that this mission was active from 1856 to 1878.

St. Patrick's Church, Sulphur Springs

After the large lumber mills cut the virgin timber from their lands in Jefferson County, they sold the tracts for whatever they could get for them. O. E. McKenzie bought considerable acreage, and divided it into smaller tracts. He advertised the land in foreign language news papers in several urban areas of the Midwest. Paul Zemek, a Czechoslovakian, bought the first land in the Lee Springs area about 2 miles west of Sulphur Springs, 18

St. Patrick's Church, Sulphur Springs, Arkansas, about 1921. Reproduction photography by Bryant.

September 1912. Others, such as Peter Bocek, John Mitosinka, and Charles Suva bought land at Lee Springs, and a Bohemian community was established. These Czechoslovakian families were joined by several other families, and at least by one Polish couple, Mary and Charles Spousta.[3]

Most of these families had limited incomes. Instead of growing cotton, these Bohemian people cultivated grapes, strawberries, vegetables and pecans, as these families had experience in this type of farming in their native lands. They also raised chickens, hogs and cattle, mostly for their own needs, but did sell some dairy products and cured meats. By the 1930's the community was selling most of their produce in Pine Bluff.[4]

St. Patrick's Church, built about 1929 was a mission of St. Joseph's Catholic Church, and the priests conducted regular services there in the 1930's and 1940's. After World War II, this Bohemian community more or less dissolved, as the younger generation moved away, and the older people could no longer farm. St. Patrick's was abandoned and dismantled[5] about 1952.[6]

Chapter 23

Parish Religious Education

The Parish Religious Education Program is established and maintained for the purpose of supplementing and supporting parents in their responsibility for the religious education of their children.[1]

The Parish Religious Education staff provides such religious instruction and spiritual growth experience, to afford the youth of the Parish attending non-Catholic schools, the opportunity to obtain knowledge of their Catholic faith and Christian values.[2]

Mrs. Paul Mayhan and Mrs. Leroy Koschel

Sister Florence Yutterman was in charge of this program until 1972, and in 1973 the school was closed. In August of 1980–82, the Parish Religious Education Program was under the able direction of Sister Maria Kleinschmidt A secretarial position was formed in 1980; this position being held for one year by Mrs. Jimmy Duck, with Mrs. Paul Mayhan the secretary since 1981.[3]

Mrs. Leroy Koschel became Director in June of 1982. Mrs. Koschel, a native of New Orleans, Louisiana is a graduate of St. Mary's Dominican High School, and received a B.S. from Dominican College, and an M.S. from St. Louis University.[4]

There are 350 students in the Parish Religious Education program for the 1983–84 school year.[5]

Chapter 24

Church Organizations

Knights of Columbus

Pine Bluff Council #1153 of the Knights of Columbus was chartered on 18 November 1906, and has served the Catholic churches of the area, as well as the community at large for 78 years.[1]

The Knights of Columbus are practicing Catholic gentlemen over the age of 18 who are bound together in a fraternal order. Third Degree Knights practice in a special manner, principles of Charity, Unity and Fraternity, and the Fourth Degree also encourages these principles, as well as Patriotism.[2] As individuals, Knights of Columbus are to be found in active roles in parishes and missions, and are often prominent in area and state roles.[3]

From the beginning, the Council has been a vital part of the community, with Knights of Columbus members participating in the various needs of the community, from offering the use of its council quarters during the tornadoes of 1947, to assisting with the Babe Ruth World Series.[4]

In 1951, the Knights of Columbus had erected at St. Joseph's Cemetery, at a cost of $1000.00, a large outside bronze crucifix, replacing one damaged by a storm. The crucifix was presented at the time to Monsignor Walshe, Pastor, in memory of the deceased members of the Pine Bluff Council.[5]

Members have been most active in the past in civic and special projects: Boy Scouts, Local Boy's Club, Boy's State and The Pilot Club. They have cooperated with Diocesan, local and national appeals for relief and charity.

The Knights of Columbus work in conjunction with the State Knights of Columbus and beginning in about 1976 began raising funds for the mentally retarded. They help Jenkins Memorial Children's Center with the Special

Knights of Columbus Officers—1984. Left to right, Mr. Dan Petrus, Treasurer, Mr. Chuck Turchi, Financial Secretary, Mr. Jeff Winkler, Deputy Grand Knight, and Mr. Michael Turchi, Grand Knight.

Olympics, as well as aiding people in many other charitable activities. They have contributed to the special Knights of Columbus Seminary Burse in the Diocese of Little Rock, St. Joseph's Orphanage, The Guardian Picture Service, The Newman Foundation, and the Monsignor W. J. Tynin Burse at St. John's Seminary.[6]

The following are Grand Knights and their terms of office:[7]

1—	Edwin J. Kerwin	1906–09/1916–18/1923–26
2—	William J. Mara	1909–10
3—	J. Frank Franey	1910–11/1918–19
4—	Jules T. Borreson	1911–13
5—	F. Knox Scull	1913–15
6—	Frank E. Dietz	1915–16
7—	Charles F. Moore	1919–21
8—	Toney Franey	1921–23
9—	Frank A. Steele	1926–28
10—	John J. Craig	1928–30
11—	John J. Holland	1930–31
12—	Frank X. Hughes	1931–33
13—	Frank B. Mitchell	1933–35
14—	Edward J. Sauter	1935–36
15—	Albert C. Ernst	1936–41
16—	Harry E. King	1941–44

17—Joseph Aull	1944–45
18—Fred I. Maher	1945–47
19—James A. McEwen	1947–48
20—J. Leo Steele	1948–50
21—William J. Cranston	1950–51
22—Neddo J. Marino	1951–53
23—Donald B. Lynch	1953–55
24—William H. King	1955–56
25—Bill Wilbert	1956–57
26—Robert J. Dempsey	1958–59
27—Tim Massanelli	1960–61
28—Vince Abbene	1962–63
29—J. Pelton Mooney	1964
30—Iggie Elkins, Sr.	1965
31—Albert Aureli	1966–67
32—Jack Diamond	1968–69
33—Benny J. Fratesi	1970
34—Dave Lupo	1971–72
35—Gil Redelman	1973
36—Dan Petrus	1974
37—J. Edwin Karlovic	1975
38—Denis Dandeneau	1976–77
39—Wadie Fakouri	1978–79
40—George D. Batzos	1980–81
41—Michael Turchi	1982–1984

Catholic Daughter's of the Americas

Court Victory 564 of the Catholic Daughters of the Americas was instituted 11 December 1921 with 62 members. At this writing, only two of the charter members survive. They are Mrs. G. H. Gaske, and Mrs. Henry Reyer.

The Catholic Daughters are presently under a seven fold program of Involvement, which includes Personal, Ecumenical, Civic, Social, Educational, Charitable and Youth programs.

Four of Court Victory's members have had the honor of serving as State Regent of the Arkansas State Court of Catholic Daughters: Mrs. Frank Steele, Mrs. Albert Ernst, Miss Agnes Moran and Mrs. John Turchi.[8]

Officers for 1983–85 are:

Mrs. Wiley Mitchell	Regent
Mrs. Charles Max Neece	1st Vice Regent
Mrs. Michael Turchi	2nd Vice Regent

Catholic Daughters of the Americas, Officers—1984. Front row, left to right, Mrs. Dean Chambliss, Treasurer, Mrs. Michael Turchi, Second Vice-Regent, Mrs. Daniel J. Petrus, Monitor. Back row, left to right, Mrs. Steve Rucker, Financial Secretary, Mrs. Charles Max Neece, First Vice-Regent, and Mrs. Wiley Mitchell, Regent.

Mrs. Harold Ward	Recording Secretary
Mrs. Steve Rucker	Financial Secretary
Mrs. Dean Chambliss	Treasurer
Mrs. Daniel J. Petrus	Monitor
Mrs. R. F. McGrath	Trustee
Mrs. Frank Turchi, Jr.	Trustee
Mrs. Don Miller	Trustee
Mrs. John Karlovic	Trustee
Mrs. R. J. Dempsey, Jr.	District Deputy

Catholic Youth Organization

The Catholic Youth Organization promotes a fourfold program of Spiritual, Cultural, Social, and Physical activity. Its membership is open to all Catholic students, grades 9 through 12. The Catholic Youth Organization has as its aim, to further the lay apostolate of the Holy Mother Church by means of observation, discussion and action.[9]

The officers for the Catholic Youth Organization are:

President	Robert Moellers

Catholic Youth Organization, Officers—1984. Seated, left to right, Miss Brynn Koshel, Secretary, Miss Brenda Culpepper, Treasurer. Standing, left to right, Mr. John Moellers, Sergeant At Arms, Mr. Chris Wood, Vice-President, Mr. Robert Moellers, President, and Mr. Tim Franklin, Sergeant At Arms.

Vice President	Chris Wood
Secretary	Brynn Koschel
Treasurer	Brenda Culpepper
Adult Advisor	Mrs. Joe Turchi

St. Joseph's Altar Society

 The oldest organization in the parish is St. Joseph's Altar Society. On arrival at St. Joseph's Church, Pine Bluff, Monsignor John M. Lucey saw the need of assistance in the care of the altar by a group of women. He called upon the women of the parish to organize, and he received a ready response. On 19 March 1873, St. Joseph's Altar Society was born.[10]

 No records can be found of the Society's earliest activities, or who comprised the initial membership. Though the members were few in number, they certainly were a faithful band of ladies to keep their society intact through the years. Except for Mrs. B. E. Benton and Mrs. A. M. Norris, who were the first to preside, the early leaders of this group are unknown to us. One distinction this early group had was the number of mothers and daughters who were enrolled; the daughters joining when they were quite young and holding that membership until death, which in several cases, was a ripe old age.[11]

Before a rectory was built, the priests attending the faithful in Pine Bluff were welcomed into the A. M. Norris home. Mrs. Norris cared for the altar needs most graciously, washing and ironing altar linens, molding candles and arranging the flowers for the Holy Sacrifice. After the inception of the Altar Society, Mrs. Norris continued these duties, sharing these honors with her niece, Mrs. Haizlip and with Mrs. Portis. Later Mrs. P. H. Pendleton took over these duties, then Mrs. W. O. Taggart, who instructed the school girls from Annunciation Academy in these essential duties. Later, Mrs. Joe White, Mrs. Mary Holland Craig, Mrs. J. L. Armfield, Mrs. Mattie Ragan, Miss Marie Aull and Mrs. Ellen Mitchell took over these duties. In 1942 it was decided to give every member of the Society the privilege of doing their part. The membership was divided into groups, each group to care for the altars during the month assigned to them.[12]

Making and repairing altar linens has always been accomplished by ready and willing hands in the Altar Society, and Sacristy needs replenished when necessary. The Altar Society from its very beginning has maintained the priests and altar boy vestments, purchased all candles used on the altars, been responsible for cleaning the sanctuary and sacristy regularly, and cleaning statues and Stations of the Cross.[13]

For several years, crews of two ladies each, contacted every Catholic family for help on the church debt, when during the depression years the Sunday collections were inadequate. These ladies also solicited, not for any gain for the Society, subscriptions to the Guardian, our Diocesan weekly paper.[14]

In the early days, bazaars were the chief source of revenue for the Altar Society, and in later years, socials and raffles have been given to raise money to carry on needed work of the Society.[15]

In the spiritual field, St. Joseph's Altar Society has two masses offered at a member's death and a mass offered for close relatives of members. On First Friday, masses are offered for the living and deceased members of the Altar Society. When death calls a member of St. Joseph's Parish, the members of the Society arrange for a complete meal for the family of the deceased, presently under the able direction of Mrs. Louis Smith.

In 1945–46, officers of the Society were (from left to right in photo): Miss Hilda Matz, Treasurer; Mrs. Paul Finkbeiner, President; Mrs. Z. F. Mitchell, Vice President; Mrs. William Puddephatt, Secretary.

By 1952, the membership list was 126 and then included the following new members:

Mrs. Louis Smith
Mrs. Stuart Pattillo
Mrs. W. J. Conery

Altar Society Officers—1945–46. Left to right, Miss Hilda Matz, Treasurer, Mrs. Paul Finkbeiner, President, Mrs. Z.F. Mitchell, Vice-President, and Mrs. William Puddephatt, Secretary.

Altar Society Officers—1983–84. Front row, left to right, Mrs. C.F. Marlo, President, Mrs. Frank Fair, Vice-President. Back row, left to right, Mrs. William Puddephatt, Treasurer, and Mrs. Lawrence Burch, Secretary.

Mrs. Wallace McGeorge
Miss Jessie Dean Southard
Mrs. A. Turchi
Mrs. Theresa Turchi
Mrs. Frances Turchi
Mrs. Joe Aureli
Mrs. Henry Bauni[16]

By 1984, the membership of St. Joseph's Altar Society reached 230 persons. Seen in photo are officers for 1983–84: President, Mrs. C. F. Marlo; Vice President, Mrs. Frank Fair; Secretary, Mrs. Lawrence Burch; and Treasurer, Mrs. William Puddephatt.

The Legion of Mary

The Legion of Mary is a world-wide organization of Catholic, men and women who offer their services to their pastor to aid him in performing spiritual works in the parish. This is done by placing themselves under the banner of Mary so that with her help they may develop greater holiness in their own lives, as well as spread a deeper devotion to her among others. Officers:

President	Mrs. C. F. Marlo
Secretary	Mrs. Neel Beasley

Chapter 25
The 1984 Parish Council: A Pictorial

The Parish Council
The Very Reverend Leo Anthony Riedmueller, V.F.
*   and*

The Parish Council Officers. Front row, left to right, Mrs. Frank Fair, Recording Secretary, and Mrs. R.F. McGrath, Vice-President. Back row, left to right, Mr. Robert Moellers, President, and Mrs. David Young, Secretary.

Chapter 26

The Staff of St. Joseph's: A Pictorial

The Staff of St. Joseph's
Mrs. Roland Barthet, Secretary

Mrs. Carl Martin, Housekeeper

Mr. Romeo Champagne, Maintenance Engineer

Chapter 27

The Organists of St. Joseph's: A Pictorial

The Organists of St. Joseph's
Left to right, Mrs. O.L. Stafford, Mrs. Tim Boeving, Mrs. J.R. Gray, and Mrs. M.D. Luneau.

FOOTNOTES

Chapter 1

Catholic Missionaries in Arkansas

1. The Catholic Church in Arkansas 1541-1843. A Dissertation for the Catholic University of America. Francis Joseph Guy (Frank Shaw Guy) Washington D.C. 1931—page 1
2. The Arkansas Mission Under Rosati—Rev. F. G. Holweck—Jefferson County Historical Quarterly, Volume 5, number 3, page 11
3. Along the Arkansas—Anna Lewis, Ph.D.,—Published 1932—Chapter I, page 13
4. Seignorial—relating or belonging to a signary or a lord. Seigniory—the territory of a lord: Domain—Webster's Dictionary—1976, page 2116
5. Along the Arkansas—Anna Lewis, Ph.D., published 1932—Chapter I, page 15
6. Tonty and The Beginning of Arkansas Post—Norman W. Caldwell. Arkansas Historical Quarterly, Volume VIII, number 3, page 190
7. The Arkansas Mission Under Rosati—Rev. F. G. Holweck, Jefferson County Historical Quarterly, volume 5, number 3, page 11
8. The Catholic Church in Arkansas 1541-1843—A Dissertation for the Catholic University of America. Francis Joseph Guy (Frank Shaw Guy) Washington D.C. 1932
9. The History of Catholicity in Arkansas 1925—The Guardian, Little Rock, Arkansas
10. The Arkansas Mission Under Rosati—Rev. F. G. Holweck—page 11—Jefferson County Historical Quarterly—Volume 5, number 3
11. Ibid—page 12
12. The History of Catholicity in Arkansas—1925—The Guardian, Little Rock, Arkansas
13. Catholic Encylopedia, Volume 6—1967—McGraw-Hill, page 464
14. The Catholic Church in Arkansas 1541-1843. A Dissertation for the Catholic University of America—Francis Joseph Guy (Frank Shaw Guy) Washington, D.C. 1932—page 55
15. The Arkansas Mission Under Rosati—Rev. F. G. Holweck—Jefferson County Historical Quarterly—Volume 5, number 3, page 12
16. The Catholic Church in Arkansas 1541-143—A Dissertation for the Catholic University of America. Francis Joseph Guy (Frank Shaw Guy) Washington, D.C. 1932 page 81
17. The Arkansas Mission Under Rosati—Rev. F. G. Holweck—Jefferson County Historical Quarterly—Volume 5, number 3, page 12
18. The History of Catholicity in Arkansas—1925—The Guardian, Little Rock, Arkansas Bishop John Rosati C. M. (Congregation of the Mission) Official title of the Vincentian Fathers. Reference: Sister Jane Frances Bey, D.C.
19. Ibid
20. The Catholic Church in Arkansas, Monsignor J. M. Lucey—1906—page 17

Chapter 2
St. Mary's Settlement

1. The Arkansas Mission Under Rosati—Rev. F. G. Holweck, Jefferson County Historical Society, Volume 5, number 3, page 12
2. Jefferson County Historical Quarterly Volume 3, number 2, page 15, A Most Historic Church—Dave Wallis
3. Ibid—pages 15–16
4. Ibid—page 16
5. Ibid
6. Ibid
7. Ibid
8. Ibid
9. The Arkansas Mission Under Rosati—Rev. F. G. Holweck—Jefferson County Historical Quarterly—Volume 5, number 3, page 25
10. Jefferson County Historical Quarterly—Volume 3, number 2, page 16—A Most Historic Church—Dave Wallis
11. The Arkansas Mission Under Rosati—Rev. F. G. Holweck—Jefferson County Quarterly, Volume 5, number 3, page 27
12. Jefferson County Historical Quarterly—Volume 3, number 2, page 16—A Most Historic Church—Dave Wallis
13. Ibid—page 17
14. Ibid
15. It is not clear to this author as to exactly what Father Dupuy had in mind by Congress land, probably he was referring to school or Seminary land set aside by the Congress. "... a great part of it (land) selected for seminary land for the use of the Territory" ... See American State Papers—Walter Lowrie—Editor—Washington, D.C.—1834—Public Lands, Volume 6, pages 22–23
16. The Arkansas Mission Under Rosati—Rev. F. G. Holweck—Jefferson County Historical Quarterly, Volume 5, number 3, pages 28–29
17. arpent—any of various old French units of land area: one used in French sections of Canada and the United States equal to about 0.85 acre. Webster's Collegiate Dictionary, page 61
18. The Arkansas Mission Under Rosati—Rev. F. G. Holweck—Jefferson County Historical Quarterly, Volume 5, number 3, page 30
19. Jefferson County Historical Quarterly, Volume 3, number 2, page 17 A Most Historic Church—Dave Wallis
20. Ibid pages 17–18
21. The Arkansas Mission Under Rosati—Rev. F. G. Holweck—Jefferson County Historical Quarterly, Volume 5, number 3, page 34
22. Ibid
23. Jefferson County Historical Quarterly, Volume 3, number 2, page 18—A Most Historic Church—Dave Wallis
24. Ibid
25. Jefferson County Historical Quarterly, 1975, Volume 6, number 3, page 35—St. Mary's Academy
26. Ibid—pages 36–37
27. Jefferson County Historical Quarterly, Volume 3, number 2, page 18—A Most Historic Church—Dave Wallis
28. Ibid
29. Jefferson County Historical Quarterly, Volume 3, number 2, page 28—The Quapaws—Dave Wallis
30. Ibid—pages 28–29
31. The History of Catholicity in Arkansas—The Guardian—1925—Little Rock, Arkansas
32. Ibid

33. Early Pine Bluff resident who wrote extensively about the area.
34. Jefferson County Historical Quarterly—Volume 6, number 2, page 28—Saracen—Dave Wallis

Chapter 3
St. Mary's Plum Bayou and Cemetery Records

1. Jefferson County Historical Quarterly, Volume 3, number 2, page 18. A Most Historic Church—Dave Wallis
2. Ibid, page 19
3. Notes from Mr. John C. Webkes, Pine Bluff, Arkansas, 1983
4. Ibid
5. See Grand Prairie History Society Bulletin—Volume 25—1982, volumes 1 and 2—Catholic Register—French Records 1831-1853

Chapter 4
St. Peter's—New Gascony and Cemetery Records

1. Jefferson County Historical Quarterly, Volume 2, number 1, page 7—New Gascony One of the Oldest Landmarks in Jefferson County—Dave Wallis
2. Ibid
3. Ibid
4. Ibid
5. Ibid
6. Ibid
7. Ibid
8. Ibid
9. The Arkansas Mission Under Rosati—Rev. F. G. Holweck, Jefferson County Historical Quarterly, Volume 5, number 3, page 35
10. Ibid
11. Arkansas Cemetery Inscriptions and Genealogical Records, Volume I—1966 compiled and edited by Counts Genealogical Research and Pub., North Little Rock, Arkansas

Chapter 5
Old French Cemetery

1. Jefferson County Historical Quarterly, Volume 7, number 3, page 15—Old French Cemetery—C. Frank Williamson
2. Ibid
3. Ibid
4. Ibid, pages 15-16
5. Ibid, page 16

Chapter 6
Early Catholic Families

1. Joseph Bonne—Mrs. Minnie Roane Tomlinson, Jefferson County Historical Quarterly, Volume 1, number 2, page 3, 1962
2. Ibid
3. Ibid
4. Ibid
5. Ibid
6. Some random notes on Antoine Barraque—C. Frank Williamson, Jefferson County Historical Quarterly, Volume 6, number 4, page 17
7. Ibid, page 18
8. Ibid
9. Ibid, page 18–19
10. Ibid, page 19
11. Father Beauprez Letters—Rev. F. G. Holweck, Jefferson County Historical Quarterly, Volume 5, number 12, page 36, 1974
12. Genealogical notes of the Valliere-Vaugine Family—Mrs. Myra Vaughan. Arkansas Historical Quarterly, Volume 15, number 4, pages 309–310
13. Centennial History of Arkansas—Dallas T. Herndon, Volume 1, page 130
14. Ibid
15. Genealogical notes of the Valliere-Vaugine Family—Mrs. Myra Vaughan. Arkansas Historical Quarterly, Volume 15, number 4, page 309
16. Ibid, page 315
17. Jefferson County Historical Quarterly, Volume 9, number 4, page 4—Emma Harris Hughes
18. Ibid
19. Ibid
20. The History of Catholicity in Arkansas—The Guardian, 1925, Little Rock, Arkansas
21. Article published by Margaret Smith Ross in the Arkansas Democrat Magazine page 1, no date on clipping—lent by Mr. John Webkes
22. Ibid, page 2
23. Arkansas Cemetery Inscriptions and Genealogical Records, Volume I, page 57, 1966
24. Article published by Margaret Smith Ross in the Arkansas Democrat Magazine, page 2, no date on clipping—lent by Mr. John Webkes
25. The Scull Letters—Dave Wallis—Jefferson County Historical Quarterly, Volume 3, number 1, page 5
26. Cemetery Records—New Gascony
27. Jefferson County Historical Quarterly, Volume I, number 3, page 18
28. Jefferson County Historical Quarterly, Volume 5, number 3

Chapter 7
St. Joseph's Church—Pullen and Georgia Streets

1. Jefferson County Historical Quarterly, 1975, Volume 6, number 1, page 8
2. Ibid
3. The History of Catholicity in Arkansas—The Guardian 1925—Little Rock, Arkansas
4. Ibid
5. Ibid

Chapter 8
St. Joseph's Church—West Sixth Avenue

1. Notes from the late Mrs. Frank Brenke
2. The History of Catholicity in Arkansas—1925, The Guardian, Little Rock, Arkansas
3. Ibid
4. Notes and photographs from Bishop Fletcher
5. Ibid
6. The Guardian, Little Rock, Arkansas, 13 November 1970
7. Ibid
8. The History of Catholicity in Arkansas—The Guardian—1925, Little Rock, Arkansas
9. Father Lucey's Handbook—1907
10. Father Lucey's Annual Report Ending December 1911
11. Report to author: Mr. John Webkes, Pine Bluff, Arkansas
12. The History of Catholicity in Arkansas—The Guardian—1925—Little Rock, Arkansas
13. Ibid
14. Ibid

Chapter 9
St. Joseph's Church—1922 to the Present Time

1. Author's notes from Mr. John Webkes
2. The History of Catholicity in Arkansas—The Guardian—1925—Little Rock, Arkansas
3. Ibid
4. Ibid
5. St. Beatrice (A.D. 304?) Of these martyrs in Rome, no reliable particulars are known. The legend relates... when brought before the judge she was ordered to sacrifice, but she replied boldly that she would do no act of worship towards demons, for she was a Christian... The relic (of this martyr) was translated by Pope St. Leo II in the seventh century to the Church of Santa Bibiana and later to St. Mary Major's. "The Lives of the Saints"—Butler, page 206—records in the Chancery Office—Diocese of Little Rock.
6. Notes by the late Mrs. Frank Brenke, Pine Bluff, Arkansas
7. Ibid
8. The History of Catholicity in Arkansas—The Guardian—1925—Little Rock Arkansas
9. Notes by the late Mrs. Frank Brenke, Pine Bluff, Arkansas
10. Ibid
11. St. Joseph's Handbook—1969, pages 13-14
12. Minutes of St. Joseph's Church—Board of Wardens meeting 1933-43
13. St. Joseph's Handbook—1969, page 14
14. Ibid
15. Minutes of St. Joseph's Church Board of Wardens—1941
16. St. Joseph's Church Handbook—1971
17. St. Joseph's Church Handbook—1969, page 14
18. Ibid
19. Notes by the late Mrs. Frank Brenke, Pine Bluff, Arkansas
20. St. Joseph's Church Handbook—1969, pages 15-16
21. Ibid, page 14
22. St. Joseph's Church Handbook, 1971
23. Ibid
24. Ibid, 1969, page 17
25. Ibid, page 14
26. Ibid
27. Ibid

28. Ibid
29. Records in the Chancery Office, Diocese of Little Rock
30. Ibid

Chapter 10
Assistant Pastors, 1908–1984

1. St. Joseph's Catholic Church Handbook, 1983

Chapter 11
Memorials

1. Information—courtesy of Mr. John Webkes, Mrs. Charles Frank Marlo, Miss Grace Allen Rike
2. This grand organ which was installed by the M. P. Moeller Organ Company of Hagerstown, Maryland in 1923 at a cost of $7,270, was valued in 1973 by this company at $49,500.
3. Pamphlet—St. Joseph's Education Fund
4. Ibid
5. Ibid
6. Ibid
7. Courtesy of Mr. John Webkes

Chapter 12
The Priests of St. Joseph's

1. Records in the Chancery Office—Diocese of Little Rock
2. Confederate Veteran—January—December 1914, Volume 22, page 566
3. Pine Bluff Commercial, Wednesday, 20 June 1914
4. Pine Bluff Commercial, Wednesday, 20 June 1914
5. Pine Bluff Commercial, 11 April 1917
6. The Guardian—Little Rock, Arkansas, Volume XXXIX—1 December 1950, Page 1
7. Ibid
8. Ibid
9. Centennial History of Arkansas—Herndon, Volume III, page 653
10. Ibid
11. Ibid
12. The Guardian—Volume XXXVII, 26 November 1948, page 1
13. The Guardian—Little Rock, Arkansas, October 1979
14. Ibid
15. Chancery Office Files—Little Rock, Arkansas
16. Ibid
17. Ibid
18. The Guardian, Little Rock, Arkansas—October 1979
19. The Guardian, Little Rock, 25 August 1961
20. Ibid
21. Ibid
22. Ibid
23. Ibid

24. Pine Bluff Commercial, 6 October 1966
25. The Guardian, Little Rock, Arkansas 25 March 1960
26. Ibid
27. Ibid
28. Ibid
29. Ibid
30. Ibid
31. Pine Bluff Commercial, 12 April 1982
32. The Guardian, Little Rock, Arkansas, 15 April 1960
33. Ibid
34. Chancery Office Files, Little Rock, Arkansas
35. Ibid
36. Ibid
37. The Guardian, Little Rock, Arkansas— 10 March 1961
38. Ibid
39. Ibid
40. Chancery Office Files, Little Rock, Arkansas
41. Notes from Father Leo A. Riedmueller to author, 1983
42. Ibid
43. The Guardian, Little Rock, Arkansas 5 May 1961
44. Chancery Office Files, Little Rock, Arkansas
45. Ibid
46. Ibid

Chapter 13

The Sisters of St. Joseph's

1. Pine Bluff Commercial 25 September 1983, page 11, by Laura Newman
2. Ibid
3. Ibid
4. Folder—St. Joseph's Church
5. Ibid
6. Ibid
7. Ibid
8. Notes in the author's files
9. Ibid

Chapter 14

The Deacons of St. Joseph's

1. Pine Bluff News— 5 November 1981
2. Ibid
3. Ibid
4. Ibid
5. Ibid
6. Ibid
7. Ibid
8. Ibid
9. Ibid
10. Ibid
11. Ibid

Chapter 15
The Priests of St. Joseph's

1. Chancery Office Files, Little Rock, Arkansas
2. Ibid
3. St. Joseph's Church Handbook 1969, page 15
4. Chancery Office Files, Little Rock, Arkansas
5. Ibid
6. Ibid
7. Notes from Mrs. Charles Rickels and The Guardian 11 June 1982
8. Official Catholic Directory and The Guardian, 20 June 1958
9. Chancery Office, Little Rock, Arkansas

Chapter 16
The Sisters from St. Joseph's

1. Random Sketches from the archives, Archival Center, Sisters of Charity of Nazareth, Nazareth, Kentucky—Sister Agnes G. McGann (1978) pages 16–17
2. St. Joseph's Handbook 1969, page 21
3. Ibid, pages 21–22
4. Archives—Sisters of Charity of Nazareth, Nazareth, Kentucky 1984
5. Ibid

Chapter 17
The Bishops of Little Rock

1. The History of Catholicity in Arkansas, The Guardian—1925
2. Ibid
3. Ibid
4. Ibid
5. Newspaper clippings gathered by the late Mrs. Frank Brenke
6. The History of Catholicity in Arkansas, The Guardian—1925
7. Ibid
8. Ibid
9. Ibid
10. Ibid
11. Ibid
12. Ibid
13. Ibid
14. Ibid
15. Ibid
16. Ibid
17. Ibid
18. Ibid
19. Ibid
20. Arkansas Gazette 23 October 1946
21. Ibid
22. Arkansas Gazette 7 December 1979
23. Ibid
24. Ibid

25. Ibid
26. Ibid
27. Ibid
28. Ibid
29. Ibid
30. Chancery Office Files—Little Rock, Arkansas
31. Ibid
32. Ibid
33. Ibid
34. Arkansas Gazette, Friday, 8 September 1972
35. Ibid
36. Ibid
37. Ibid
38. Ibid
39. Ibid

Chapter 18

Annunciation Academy, St. Joseph's School, Pine Bluff Catholic School and Convent Chapel

1. The History of Catholicity in Arkansas—The Guardian—1925
2. Ibid
3. Ibid
4. Ibid
5. Ibid
6. Ibid
7. St. Joseph's Catholic Church Handbook—1983
8. Ibid
9. Ibid
10. St. Joseph's Catholic Church Handbook—1969
11. Ibid
12. St. Joseph's Catholic Church Handbook—1971
13. The Guardian—27 April 1973
14. Ibid
15. Notes from the parish office

Chapter 19

St. Joseph's Cemetery and Interments 1840–1913

1. Notes from Mr. John Webkes
2. Ibid
3. Ibid
4. Daniel Carroll II—One Man and His Descendents 1730-1978—Sr. Virginia Geiger, Ph.D., page 82
5. World Book Encyclopedia—1966—Volume 3, page 185
6. Notes from Mr. John Webkes
7. Ibid
8. Ibid
9. Letters of Monsignor Walshe to Bishop Fletcher 7 September 1947
10. Notes from Mr. John Webkes

Chapter 20
Laymen of St. Joseph's

1. Fine Bluff Commercial 4 June 1979
2. Pine Bluff Commercial 21 April 1976
3. Ibid
4. Ibid
5. Pine Bluff Commercial 21 September 1969
6. Pine Bluff Graphic 10 December 1927
7. Pine Bluff Commercial 27 August 1981
8. Pine Bluff Graphic 15 September 1909

Chapter 21
St. Peter's Mission

1. The History of Catholicity in Arkansas—The Guardian—1925—Little Rock, Arkansas
2. Ibid
3. Ibid
4. St. Peter's Catholic Church—Diamond Jubilee Handbook—14 October 1973
5. The History of Catholicity in Arkansas—1925—The Guardian, Little Rock, Arkansas
6. Archives of the Diocese of Little Rock, Arkansas
7. The History of Catholicity in Arkansas—1925—The Guardian, Little Rock, Arkansas
8. Ibid
9. Ibid
10. St. Peter's Catholic Church Handbook, 1973

Chapter 22
Blessed Sacrament, Grady and Cemetery Records, St. Paul's, Noble Lake and St. Patrick's, Sulphur Springs

1. St. Joseph's Handbook—1983
2. Deedbook F, page 491, Jefferson County Court House
3. Pine Bluff Commercial 15 April 1974, page 13
4. Ibid
5. Ibid
6. Ibid

Chapter 23
Parish Religious Education

1. Notes from Mrs. Leroy Koschel
2. Ibid
3. Ibid
4. Ibid
5. Ibid

Chapter 24
Church Organizations

1. Notes from Mr. John Webkes
2. Ibid
3. Ibid
4. Ibid
5. St. Joseph's Handbook—1971
6. Ibid
7. Notes from Mr. John Webkes
8. St. Joseph's Handbook—1971
9. Ibid
10. Notes from the late Mrs. Frank Brenke, Pine Bluff, Arkansas
11. Ibid
12. Ibid
13. Ibid
14. Ibid
15. Ibid
16. Ibid

Chapter 25
The 1984 Parish Council

Reproductions of photographs by Bryant Photography—Pine Bluff, Ark.

Chapter 26
The Staff of St. Joseph's

Reproductions of photographs by Bryant Photography—Pine Bluff, Ark.

Chapter 27
The Organists of St. Joseph's

Reproductions of photographs by Bryant Photography—Pine Bluff, Ark.

INDEX

A

Aaronson, Mrs. Ed p. 50
Abbene, Mrs. Anna p. 50
Abbene, Antonio p. 50
Abbene, Carl p. 68
Abbene, Joseph p. 122
Abbene, Vince p. 148
Abbey, St. Bernard's, St. Bernard, Alabama p. 76
Abdallah, Mrs. Catherine p. 50
Abdallah, Jarouis p. 50
Abdallah, John p. 50
Abdallah, Mrs. Lavinia p. 50
Academies
  Academy p. 49
  Annunciation Academy p. 49, 60, 62, 95, 98, 103, 116, 119, 151
  Annunciation Academy,—circa.1903 p. 117 (illus.)
  Annunciation Academy, Students of p. 118 (illus.)
  Mt. St. Mary's Academy p. 82
  Mt. St. Mary's Academy, Little Rock p. 103
  Providence Academy, Texarkana p. 80
  St. Ambrose Academy p. 20
  St. Mary's Academy p. 19, 20
  St. Peter's Academy p. 139
  Ward's Academy p. 71
Adams, James Eugene p. 122
Adams, Mrs. Ross p. 50
Adelaide, Sister p. 103
Administrative Assistant to the Speaker of the House p. 93
Air Corps, United States Naval p. 95
Alabama p. 76, 88
Alabama, Mobile p. 73, 87

Albany, Bishop of p. 105
Alcorn, Mrs. M. T. p. 24
Alexandria, Bishop of p. 64, 81
Allen, Mrs. Gerelda p. 50
Altar, Main p. 57
Altar, Main and Altar of Sacrifice p. 59 (illus.)
Altar, Sacrifice of the Cross p. 63
America p. 17
Americas, Catholic Daughters of the p. 67, 148
Americas, Catholic Daughters of the— Officers p. 149 (illus.)
Annie Rebecca p. 122
Antoine, Gabe p. 122
Antoine, Paul p. 122
Antwine, Mrs. p. 24
Arkansas p. 11, 15, 16, 17, 20, 35, 37
Arkansas—cities
  Armstrong Springs, Ark. p. 110
  Atkins, Ark. p. 74
  El Dorado, Ark. p. 76
  Fayetteville, Ark. p. 74
  Forrest City, Ark. p. 78
  Fort Smith, Ark. p. 61, 72, 86, 88
  Grady, Ark. p. 73
  Helena, Ark. p. 105, 107
  Hot Springs, Ark. p. 74, 108
  Jonesboro, Ark. p. 74
  Little Rock, Ark. p. 15, 73, 107, 110
  Morrilton, Ark. p. 64, 82
  Napoleon, Ark. p. 29
  New Gascony, Ark p. 16
  Paris, Ark. p. 110
  Pine Bluff, Ark. p. 9, 121, 122, 136, 137, 138, 143, 151
  Pocahontas, Ark. p. 74
  Slovactown, Ark. p. 76

Stuttgart, Ark   p. 121
Texarkana, Ark   p. 79
Tontitown, Ark.   p. 110
Arkansas, Bishops of   p. 11
Arkansas, Catholics of   p. 107
Arkansas, Catholic Church in   p. 13
Arkansas, Catholic Church in the State of   p. 7
Arkansas, Catholic Missionaries in   p. 13
Arkansas—Counties
   Arkansas County, Ark.   p. 13, 18, 120
   Jefferson County, Ark.   p. 17, 18, 19, 31, 34, 37, 38, 39, 120, 138
   Union County, Ark.   p. 137
Arkansas, District of   p. 35
Arkansas—Missouri Association of Tax Representatives   p. 137
Arkansas, Noble Lake   p. 37
Arkansas Post   p. 7, 13, 14, 15, 20, 33, 35, 137
Arkansas, Post of   p. 35
Arkansas, Quapaw Indian chiefs in   p. 121
Arkansas, State of   p. 15, 105, 110
Armfield, Ivy, family   p. 69
Arnfield, Mrs. J. L.   p. 151
Armfield, Mrs. Mary   p. 50
Army, Confederate   p. 71
Army, United States   p. 61
Arpent—Chapter 2, #17   p. 160
Arsenal, Pine Bluff   p. 137
Association, Ark. Bus & Truck   p. 91
Association, Ark. Movers   p. 91
Association, First South Federal Savings & Loan   p. 93
Aull, Mrs. Clara   p. 69
Aull, Joseph   p. 148
Aull, Miss Marie   p. 151
Aureli, Mr. Al   p. 95
Aureli, Albert   p. 148
Aureli, Dominick   p. 122
Aureli, family   p. 68
Aureli, Mrs. Joe   p. 153
Aureli, Louis and Bass, family   p. 119
Aureli, Father Michael   p. 68
Aureli, The Rev. Michael Valentine   p. 94 (illus.), 95
Aureli, Mrs.   p. 95

B

Babcock, Herbert   p. 122
Babcock, Mrs. Nora   p. 122
Baccarossa, Infant   p. 122
Bachman, Sister Patricia, D.C.   p. 85 (illus.)
Baldwin, J.   p. 50
Balo, Mrs.   p. 50
Baltz, Father Al   p. 66
Baltz, Father Guy   p. 66
Bank, Citizen's   p. 41

Barbler, Joseph   p. 122
Barbler, Mrs. Josie   p. 122
Barnes, Emma Lehnert   p. 118 (illus.)
Barranco, Charles, family   p. 69
Barraque, Antoine   p. 19, 28, 31, 34 (illus.), 35
Barraque, Gustave   p. 122
Barraque, Mary Therese Dardenne   p. 35
Barraque, Monsieur   p. 34
Barrens, Seminary of the   p. 107
Barthet, Mrs. Rowland   p. 11, 118, 156 (illus.)
Bartholomew, Lewis   p. 39
Basilica, Lateran, Rome   p. 108
Basilica, St. Peter's   p. 96
Bauer, Father Ralph   p. 66
Bauni, Mrs. Henry   p. 153
Baxter and Brooks   p. 107
Bayou, Brump's   p. 121
Bayou, Plum   p. 22
Bazaar   p. 46
Bateman, Mrs. Delbert   p. 118
Batterton, Infant   p. 122
Batzos, George D.   p. 148
Batzos, the James, family   p. 119
Beasley, Mrs. Neel   p. 153
Beatrice, Saint   p. 57
Beauprez, Father   p. 16, 17, 18
Beauprez, Father Pierre   p. 16
Beauprez, P. F.   p. 17
Begley, Mrs. Fannie   p. 122
Begley, William J.   p. 122
Behan, Rev. P.   p. 71
Bell and Bocage   p. 45
Belluomini, G.   p. 123
Bennett, Mr.   p. 123
Benton, Mrs. B. E.   p. 50, 150
Benton, Mrs. B. W.   p. 50
Benton, Miss Eulalia   p. 50
Benton, Eulalie W.   p. 67
Benton, Mrs. Margaret E.   p. 67
Beomis, Florence   p. 43
Berry, Mrs. D.   p. 123
Beunet, Ann Myrtle   p. 123
Bey, Sister Jane Frances, D.C.   p. 84 (illus.), 86 (illus.)
Biancalana, Mrs. Louisa   p. 50
Biancalana, M.   p. 50
Biancalana, Valentine   p. 50
Bishop, Mrs. Anna   p. 50
Bishop, Auxiliary of Little Rock   p. 81
Bishop, Etta   p. 123
Bishop, Harry   p. 123
Bishop, Wilford Joseph   p. 123
Bishop, Ruby   p. 118
Bishop, W.   p. 50
Bishop, Mrs. W. A.   p. 54
Black, John Thomas   p. 123

Blackburn, James p. 123
Blanchard, Charles p. 123
Blanchard, Mrs. George p. 123
Bland, C.B. p. 50
Bland, Mrs. Josephine p. 50
Blaney, Mrs. Caroline p. 123
Blaney, G. M. p. 123
Board, Clergy Personnel p. 83
Board, Diocesan Personnel p. 82
Board, Jefferson Co. Equilization p. 137
Board, St. Joseph's School p. 136
Bocage, J. M. p. 138
Bocage, Judge p. 21
Bocek, Peter p. 143
Boeving, Mrs. Tim p. 158 (illus.)
Boggins, Mary p. 123
Bogy, Ataline p. 20
Bogy, Catherine p. 37
Bogy, Charles p. 15
Bogy, F. p. 20
Bogy, family p. 37
Bogy, Ignatius p. 39
Bogy, Joseph (Dr.) p. 123
Bogy, L. p. 20
Bogy, Louis p. 16
Bogy, Malelda p. 20
Bogy, Matilda p. 20
Bogy, Teresa p. 24
Bolued, John p. 123
Bond, Infant p. 123
Bond, Josephine p. 123
Bond, Mildred p. 123
Bonne, Baptiste p. 39
Bonne, Joseph p. 33, 34 (illus.)
Bonne, Joseph, Sr. p. 31
Bonne, Michael p. 33
Boone, Mary C. p. 37
Bord , Agnes p. 20
Boreson, Jules T. p. 50
Boreson, Mrs. Jules T. p. 50
Borrensen, Jules T. p. 54, 147
Boswell, family p. 69
Boyce, Elizabeth p. 69
Boyce, Mrs. Elizabeth p. 50
Boyce, Helen p. 119
Boyce, Infants p. 123
Boyce, Mrs. J. E. p. 123
Boyce, Joseph p. 50
Boyce, Miss Kate p. 54
Boyce, Miss Mary p. 50
Boyd's Point p. 38
Boyle, John p. 69
Bradford, H. P. p. 121
Bradley, John p. 123
Bradley, Mrs. p. 50
Bradshaw, Theodosia Malvina p. 29
Bradshaw, W. H. p. 29
Bramber, Mary p. 20

Bramber, R. p. 20
Brenke, Anthony p. 50
Brenke, Bernard S. p. 123
Brenke, Mr. & Mrs. F. H. p. 70
Brenke, Mrs. Frances p. 50
Brenke, Francis, Jr. p. 50
Brenke, Francis, Sr. p. 50
Brenke, Mr. & Mrs. Frank p. 136
Brenke, Mrs. Frederic p. 50
Brenke, Henry p. 50
Brenke, Infant p. 123
Brenke, John p. 50
Brenke, Mr. John B. p. 136
Brenke, Joe p. 50
Brenke, Miss Mary p. 50
Brenke, Miss Pauline p. 50
Brennan, Miss Bridget p. 50
Brennan, D. J. p. 50
Brennan, James p. 123
Brennan, Mamie p. 123
Brennan, Mrs. Norma p. 50
Brennan, Mrs. Sarah p. 50, 123
Brent, Ruby p. 118
Brick, Malvern p. 57
Brinsback, Antoine p. 15
Brooks and Baxter p. 107
Brooks, Clemence p. 20
Brooks, Elizabeth p. 19
Brooks, James p. 24
Brooks, Mary C. p. 24
Brooks, Robert p. 15, 19, 24
Brooks, William p. 25
Brown, Annie Jewell p. 123
Brown, Juanita p. 118
Brown, Mrs. p. 123
Bruce, M. M., Mr. p. 57
Bryant, Miss Catherine p. 50
Bryant, Charles p. 50
Bryant, Mrs. Isabella p. 50
Bryant, Miss Mabel p. 50
Bryant, Mr. Noel p. 11
Bryant, Percy p. 50
Bryant, Reproduction Photography by p. 44, 46, 47, 49
Bryant, R. M., family p. 69
Buck, Eugenia E. p. 20
Buck, Infant p. 123
Buck, James p. 20
Buck, Mrs. Thomas E. p. 123
Buckingham, Mrs. Nora p. 123
Bullard, Emma May p. 123
Bullard, John p. 123
Bulletin, Grand Prairie Historical Society p. 29
Burch, Mrs. Lawrence p. 153
Burdick, Infant p. 123
Bureau, Ark. Household Goods Carriers p. 91

172

Burgan, Thomas p. 123
Burke, Father William J. p. 61, 66
Burks, Reed—Willis, and p. 63
Burks, Willard, Mr. p. 63
Burton, Adell p. 25
Burton, R. M. p. 25
Burton, Sydney p. 25
Burton, Virginia p. 25
Busic, Mrs. Scott p. 50
Byrne, Bishop p. 15, 20, 107
Byrne, Bishop Andrew p. 43, 107, 142
Byrne, The Most Reverend Andrew, D.D. p. 15, 105, 106 (illus.)

C

Cady, John Andrew p. 123
Cady, Bridget Wright p. 123
Cady, family p. 68, 70
Cady, John p. 123
Cady, John Francis p. 123
Calhoun, E. H. p. 123
Calhoun, Eva May p. 123
Calhoun, Lizzie Maria p. 123
California p. 88
California, Palo Alto p. 92
California, San Francisco p. 77, 78
Cammick, Miss p. 20
Campbell, James p. 123
Canada, Montreal p. 14
Cannon, Mrs. Julia p. 67
Carle, Elizabeth p. 37
Carroll, Charles p. 121
Carroll, Daniel p. 121
Carroll, David Williamson p. 123
Carroll, D. W. p. 45
Carroll, Eleanora p. 43
Carroll, Felicia p. 43
Carroll, Bishop John p. 121
Carroll, William p. 121, 123
Cartwright, Mrs. Belle p. 124
Cartwright, G. E. p. 124
Cartwright, Mrs. p. 124
Carver, Mrs. Leonard p. 124
Casey, Father p. 65
Cathedral, Rector of the p. 108
Cathedrals
   St. Andrew's—Little Rock p. 74, 75, 78, 80, 82, 105, 107, 112
   St. John the Baptist, Savannah, Ga p. 112
   St. Patrick's—New York City p. 105
Catholics p. 18, 19, 28
Caulk, Maggie E. (Taylor) p. 29
Caulk, S. V. p. 29
Cavalier, Father John p. 14
Cavette, Father p. 14
Cemeteries
   Blessed Sacrament—Grady p. 140, 141 (illus.)
   Blessed Sacrament—Jonesboro p. 75
   Calvary—Fort Smith p. 78
   Catholic p. 120
   Graceland p. 63, 79, 122
   Old French p. 31, 32
   Pine Bluff (old) p. 21
   St. Joseph's p. 21, 120, 121, 122–135, 146
   St. Mary's—Plum Bayou p. 24, 25 (illus.), 26, 27
   St. Peter's—New Gascony p. 29–30
Center, Civic, Pine Bluff p. 49
Center, De Paul Family p. 85
Center, Jefferson Regional Medical p. 93
Center, Jenkins Memorial Children's p. 146
Cerder (?), Tim p. 124
Chalhenpe (?), Mrs. Catherine p. 124
Chambliss, Mrs. Dean p. 149
Chamberlain, Papal p. 78, 81, 112
Champagne, Romeo, Mr. p. 157 (illus.)
Chancellor p. 110
Chancellor, Diocese of Savannah p. 112
Chaney, Father Jesse p. 61
Chapel, Convent p. 116, 119
Chapel, St. Anthony's p. 49
Chaplain, Our Lady of Nazareth Home p. 82
Charlan (?), Margaret p. 124
Charlevoix, Father p. 14
Charity, Daughters of p. 86, 87, 88
Charity, Sisters of—Nazareth, Kentucky. p. 103, 107
Cheney, Father Jesse C. p. 66
Cherot, Francis p. 50
Chestnut, Charles p. 124
Chestnutt, Mrs. Annie p. 50
Chestnutt, Charlie p. 50
Chestnutt, Miss Fay p. 50
Chestnutt, John Francis p. 124
Chestnutt, Miss Leta p. 50
Chestnutt, Rudolph p. 50
Chestnutt, Talbot p. 50
Chicago, Bishop of p. 105
Children, Rescuer of Captive p. 21
Childress, Miss Amanda p. 50
Childress, Infant p. 124
Childress, Marie p. 124
Childress, Miss Nellie p. 50
Childress, Mrs. Nettie p. 50
Childress, Thelma p. 124
Childress, Miss Thelma p. 50
Childress, Thomas B. p. 124
Childress, Williamette p. 124
Childress, W. J., Dr. p. 124
Chilson, Infant p. 124
Choir, the p. 69
Chowning, James J. p. 41
Church, Catholic p. 17, 28
Church, First Methodist p. 40
Church, General Council of the p. 107

Church, Location of the second Catholic Building p. 40 (illus.)
Church, Methodist p. 21
Church, St. Mary's Bell Tower p. 24 (illus.)
Church, St. Joseph's p. 58 (illus.)
Church, St. Joseph's circa 1868 p. 41 (illus.)
Church, St. Joseph's circa 1871 p. 44 (illus.)
Church, St. Joseph's, circa 1888 p. 45 (illus.)
Church, St. Joseph's, circa 1921 p. 58 (illus.)
Church, St. Joseph's Church Societies p. 49
Churches
   Blessed Sacrament—Grady Ark. p. 60, 140
   Blessed Sacrament—Jonesboro, Ark. p. 74
   Blessed Sacrament—Savannah, Ga. p. 112
   Christ The King—Fort Smith, Ark. p. 79
   Church of the Nativity—New York City, N.Y. p. 105
   Holy Cross—Crossett, Ark. p. 82
   Holy Redeemer—El Dorado, Ark. p. 59, 74, 76, 78
   Immaculate Conception—Fort Smith, Ark. p. 78, 79, 80
   Immaculate Conception—North Little Rock, Ark. p. 64, 82
   Our Lady of Hope—Hope, Ark. p. 74
   Our Lady of the Holy Souls—Little Rock, Ark. p. 82
   Our Lady of Lourdes, Port Wentworth, Ga. p. 112
   Sacred Heart—Morrilton, Ark. p. 82
   St. Ambrose p. 15
   St. Andrew's—New York City, N.Y. p. 105
   Sts. Cyril and Methodius—Slovactown, Ark. p. 76
   St. Edwards's—Texarkana, Ark. p. 82
   St. James—New York City, N.Y. p. 105
   St. Joseph's—Fayetteville, Ark. p. 78, 83
   St. Joseph's—Hot Springs, Ark. p. 74, 82
   St. Joseph's—Pine Bluff, Ark. p. 21, 40, 41, 44, 49, 57, 60, 83, 91, 95, 96, 103, 116, 117, 119, 137, 143
   St. Joseph's—Tontitown, Ark. p. 78
   St. Mary's p. 37
   St. Mary's—Charleston, S. C. p. 105
   St. Mary's—Helena, Ark. p. 74, 76
   St. Mary's—Plum Bayou, Ark. p. 22, 23, 24, 33
   St. Patrick's—Columbus, Ohio p. 107
   St. Patrick's—North Little Rock, Ark. p. 76, 82
   St. Patrick's—Sulphur Springs, Ark. p. 140, 142, 143 (illus.)
   St. Paul's—Noble Lake, Ark. p. 37, 140, 142
   St. Paul's—Pocahontas, Ark. p. 76
   St. Peter's—New Gascony, Ark. p. 28, 29, 30, 37, 38, 39
   St. Peter's—Pine Bluff, Ark. p. 49, 85, 138
   St. Peter's—Wynne, Ark. p. 64, 82
   St. Stephen p. 14, 15
   St. Theresa's—Little Rock, Ark. p. 64, 83
Clague, Mrs. Emma p. 50
Clague, Infant p. 124
Clark, George Rogers p. 14
Clarke, Father p. 43
Clarke, P. I. Rev. p. 41, 71
Claxton, Virgil p. 124
Clay, Mrs. Elizabeth p. 124
Cling, Mrs. Angelina p. 124
Cloyes, Caroline Lutecia p. 31
Cloyes, E. L. p. 31
Cloyes, N. H. p. 31
Cloyes, Thomas Nathan p. 31
Club, Boy's p. 146
Club, Lucey p. 67
Club, the Pilot p. 146
Club, Rotary p. 137
Coadjutor p. 108
Cobb, Fanny p. 124
Cobbs, Mrs. Virginia p. 25
Colgan, Charles p. 50
Colgan, John p. 50
Colgan, Miss Julia p. 50
Collection, Lites—Wallis p. 23
Collection, Trimble p. 38
Colleges & Universities
   American College—Rome, Italy p. 74
   Arkansas, University of, at Fayetteville p. 97
   Baltimore, University of p. 112
   Catholic University, Washington, D. C. p. 80
   Chicago, University of p. 110
   Creighton University, Omaha, Neb. p. 98
   Dallas, University of p. 95, 96
   Dominican College p. 145
   Drury College, Springfield, Missouri p. 93
   Fordham University p. 72
   Fontbonne College, St. Louis, Mo. p. 87
   Georgetown University p. 121
   Gregorian University p. 80
   Holy Ghost Preparatory College p. 78
   Jesuit College, Mungreth, Ireland p. 73
   Jesuit College, Rome, Italy p. 98
   Lateran University, Rome, Italy p. 112
   Little Rock College p. 75, 108, 110
   Little Rock University p. 91
   Loyola University, New Orleans, La. p. 95
   Marquette College, Milwaukee, Wisconsin p. 98
   Memphis State University p. 91
   Minnesota, University of p. 92
   Mount St. Mary's, Baltimore, Maryland p. 73

Mount St. Mary's, Emmitsburg, Maryland p. 107
Mount St. Mary's of the West, Cincinnati, Ohio p. 107
North American College, Rome, Italy p. 80, 108
Pontifical Gregorian University, Rome, Italy p. 95
Southern California, University of p. 95
Subiaco College p. 74
St. Andrew's College, Fort Smith p. 71
St. Louis University p. 88, 145
St. Mary's College, Lebanon, Kentucky p. 108
St. Meinrad School of Theology p. 96
St. Thomas College, Milwaukee, Wis. p. 110
Temple University p. 78
Texas, University of, Arlington p. 87
University, Propaganda de Fide p. 76
Urban College De Propaganda Fide p. 108
Collet, Estelle p. 124
Collins, Mabel p. 124
Collins, Mike p. 25
Collins, Tim p. 124
Colony, St. Lawrence River p. 33
Columbus, Knights of p. 115, 136, 137, 146
Columbus, Knights of, Officers p. 147 (illus.)
Columbus, Knights of, Seminary Burse p. 147
Columbus, State Knights of p. 146
Commission, Arkansas History p. 38
Commission, Pine Bluff Parks p. 137
Committee, Arkansas Historic Preservation p. 22
Community, Bohemian p. 143
Company, Arkansas Power and Light p. 137
Company, Catholic Publication p. 108
Company, Holsum Baking p. 93
Company, T and N. Electric p. 136
Comstock, Dudley p. 50
Comstock, Julia p. 124
Comstock, Mrs. Mary p. 50
Condon, Infant p. 124
Conery, Mr. and Mrs. George A. p. 69
Conery, Mrs. W. J. p. 151
Conesso, Joseph p. 124
Confederation, Articles of p. 121
Confirmation, Sacrament of p. 43
Congregation of the Mission,Chapter 1, #18 (footnote) p. 159
Congress, Continental p. 121
Congressland, Chapter 2, #15 (footnote) p. 160
Conlan, Mrs. Mary p. 50
Conly, Idelia p. 124
Conley, J. p. 50
Conrod, the C. S. family p. 119
Consultor, Vice General and p. 81

Convent, Our Lady of Mercy, St. Louis, Mo. p. 103
Conyers, Mrs. Maggie p. 50
Conyers, Walter G. p. 124
Conyers, W. G. p. 50
Cook, Charles p. 50, 69
Cook, Mrs. Charles p. 124
Cook, Joe p. 50
Cook, Lawrence p. 124
Cook, Theresa p. 69
Cook, Mrs. Theresa p. 50
Coosotte, F. p. 31
Coosotte, C. p. 31
Coosotte, Felicity p. 32
Coosotte, Joseph Francis p. 31
Coosotte, Margaret p. 31
Coosotte, P. p. 31
Coosotte, Mrs. Sam p. 25
Coosotte, Stephen p. 31
Corder, Mrs. A. P. p. 124
Corder, Miss Lily p. 50
Corder, Mrs. Lula p. 50
Corder, Mrs. Tim p. 124
Cornestone, laying of the p. 60 (illus.)
Corps, Peace p. 97
Correnti, Reverend Joseph p. 115
Costello, John p. 124
Cosotte, Mrs. John p. 124
Cotter, Claude p. 50
Cotter, Edmund p. 50
Cotter, Miss Ellen p. 50
Cotter, Mrs. Mary p. 50
Council, the City p. 122
Council, K. of C p. 119
Council, Parish p. 136, 154, 155 (illus.)
Council, Superior of Louisiana p. 14
Council, Vatican p. 107
Counseling, Spiritual p. 89
Coupot, Francis p. 39
Court, Victory number 564 p. 68
Coussot, Francis p. 31
County, Jefferson, Dept. of Public Welfare p. 137
County, Jefferson—Pine Bluff Kiwanis Club p. 137
County, Jefferson, Tuberculosis Association p. 137
Cox, Mrs. p. 124
Craig, Mrs. Mary Holland p. 151
Craig, John J. p. 147
Craig, John J., family p. 68
Cranston, D. J. p. 50
Cranston, Mrs. Ellen p. 50
Cranston, William J. p. 148
Cratin, family p. 68
Cross, Stations of the p. 57, 59, 151
Crowley, John p. 50
Crubin, Mary p. 43

Crusade, the Catholic Student Mission p. 119
Crutcher, Jack p. 118 (illus.)
Crutcher, W. J., family p. 69, 70
Culpepper, Brenda p. 150
Cummins, Mr. p. 15
Curro, Angelo p. 50
Customs, Spanish p. 35

D

Dabb, Mrs. p. 25
Dagle, Nancy p. 20
Daigle, Francois p. 15
Daley, Mrs. Carolina p. 51
Daley, H. H. p. 51
Daley, Jerry p. 124
Dandeneau, Denis p. 148
Dardanne, Margaret p. 25
Dardenne, America G. p. 29
Dardenne, Mary Therese p. 34
Dardenne, Stanislaus p. 29, 39
Daroux, Alma Emma Louise p. 124
Daroux, Arthur p. 51
Daroux, B. J. p. 51
Daroux, Ernest p. 51
Daroux, George p. 51
Daroux, Mrs. Harriet p. 51
Daugherty, Cardinal Dennis, Archbishop of Philadelphia p. 61
Davion, Father p. 14
Davis, Anthony H. p. 41
Davis, Mrs. Caroline p. 124
Davis, Francis T. p. 25
Davis, George p. 124
Davis, J. T. p. 54
Davis, Mrs. Victoria p. 51
Dawson, Henry S. p. 41
Day, All Saints p. 139
Deaneries—Arkansas
  Little Rock Deanery p. 83
  Northwest Deanery p. 78
  Southeast Deanery p. 59, 64, 78, 79, 82, 83
Deans, Eucharist of Ordination of Permanent p. 91
De Bona, Mr. & Mrs. F. V. p. 68
Dechase, Mrs. p. 25
Decree, the Second Vatican Council's p. 68
de Carondelet , Baron—Gov. of La. p. 35
Delaney, James p. 124
Delaney, Mary p. 124
de La Salle, Robert Cavalier Sieur p. 13
Delivery, City, Inc. p. 91
Dellman, Miss Bertha p. 51
Dellman, Charles p. 51
Dellman, Miss Ethel p. 51
Dellman, Mrs. Hazel p. 51
Dellman, J. H. p. 51, 124
Dellman, Mrs. J. H. Sr. p. 124
Dellman, John H. p. 55
Dellman, Margaret p. 124
Dellman, Mrs. Mary p. 51
de Montigny, Father p. 14
de Moran, Marie Felicite p. 35
Dempsey, Miss Clara p. 51
Dempsey, Mrs. Mary p. 51, 69
Dempsey, Mrs. R. J., Jr. p. 149
Dempsey, Robert p. 51
Dempsey, Robert J. p. 148
Dennis, Mary E. p. 140
Dennison, Albert p. 124
Denny, Thomas p. 124
Dent, Mrs. Mary E. p. 25
Depatie, Fred p. 51
de Paul, The Daughters of Charity of Saint Vincent p. 84
Depression p. 61
Depression, Great p. 60
De Prima, Mrs. Frances p. 51
De Prima, Michael p. 51
Derreseaux, Andrew p. 19
Derreseaux, Jane p. 19
Derreseaux, Janette p. 19
Derreseaux, Paul p. 19
Derreseaux, Theresa p. 19
Derreuisseaux, Audile p. 25
Derreuisseaux, Alice p. 25
Derreuisseaux, Cecilia p. 25
Derreuisseaux, Eleanor p. 25
Derreuisseaux, Elizabeth p. 25
Derreuisseaux, Frances B. p. 25
Derreuisseaux, Frankie X. p. 25
Derreuisseaux, Hypolite p. 26
Derreuisseaux, Mrs. Joe p. 25
Derreuisseaux, John B. p. 26
Derriseaux, J. B. 124
Derrisieux, Mrs. Mary p. 125
Derrisseaux, Mrs. Mary p. 51
Derriusseaux, Lulie A. p. 26
Desruisseaux, Audile p. 36
Desruisseaux, Mathilde p. 36
Deshay, Robert p. 26
de Soto, Hernando p. 13
de Tonti p. 33
de Tonti's Fort p. 14
de Tonti, Henri p. 14
de Vaugine, Francois Nuisment p. 36
de Villmont, Catherine Bogy p. 37
de Villmont, Don Carlos p. 37
Diamond, Mrs. Ann p. 26
Diamond, Father Charles S. p. 61, 65
Diamond, Jack p. 148
Diamond, John W. p. 26
Diamond, Joseph p. 26
Diamond, W. M. p. 26

Dickerson, Mary p. 20
Dickerson, T. p. 20
Dienert, Father Robert p. 66
Dieticta (?) J. C. p. 125
Dietz, Frank E. p. 147
Dietz, Joseph p. 125
Diocese, Little Rock, Missionary Priests of the p. 68
Diocese, Vicar General of the p. 110
Diocese, Vice Chancellor of p. 110
Director, Spiritual p. 82
District, Arkansas p. 37
Dodge, Charles Earl p. 125
Dodge, Etiennette p. 29
Dodge, Etinette Vaugine p. 36
Dodge, John p. 19, 29, 36, 37, 39
Dodge, Louise p. 19
Dodge, Pearl p. 125
Doherty, Infant p. 125
Dolan, John p. 51
Doll, John, Jr. p. 83
Dollarton, Father F. X. p. 65
Dolors, The Seven p. 82
Donahue, Father Thomas J. p. 64, 66
Donnelly, Father p. 18, 19, 29
Donnelly, Father Peter p. 18
Donnelly, Mr. p. 19
Donelson, Annie Louise p. 26
Donovan, Mrs. Aleen p. 51
Donovan, Allien Eliza p. 125
Donovan, Mrs. Eliza p. 125
Donovan, Infant p. 125
Donovan, John p. 51, 125
Donovan, Mrs. John p. 125
Donovan, Mae p. 51
Donovan, Malachi p. 125
Donovan, Mrs. Malachi p. 125
Donovan, Mrs. Mary p. 51
Donovan, Matt p. 51
Donovan, Rev. Thomas p. 71
Doran, Ed p. 51
Doran, John p. 51
Doroux, Mrs. E. p. 125
Douay, Father p. 14
Dowd, James p. 51, 125
Dowd, Miss Nellie p. 51
Dowling, David p. 51
Downing, Evaline p. 20
Doyle, Annie p. 125
Doyle, Bridget p. 125
Doyle, Dennis p. 125
Doyle, John p. 125
Doyle, Joseph Thomas p. 125
Doyle, Patrick p. 125
Doyle, T. M. p. 55
Drake, James p. 51
Dubourg, Bishop p. 15
Duchassin, Antoine p. 39

Duck, Mrs. Jimmy p. 145
Duelmer, Clara Regina p. 125
Dugan, Andrew George p. 26
Dugan, Arthur p. 125
Dugan, Caroline p. 20, 26
Dugan, John p. 125
Dugan, Mr. p. 20
Dugan, Noble p. 26
Dugan, Petronella p. 26
Dugan, Richard N. p. 26
Duggan, Father p. 137
Duggan, Infants (twins) p. 125
Duggan, the Rev. John B. p. 45
Duggan, the Rev. John P. p. 71
Duggan, Stephen p. 125
Dulmer, Nellie p. 125
Dunn, Sister Mary Catherine, D.C. p. 86, 87 (illus.)
Du Poisson, Father p. 14
Dupuy, Father p. 17, 18, 19, 29, 35
Dupuy, Father Annemond p. 17
Durner, Andrew p. 125
Durner, Bessie p. 125
Durner, Mrs. Mary p. 51
Durrin, Henry p. 51
Dutlinger, John p. 125
Dutlinger, William p. 125
Dwyer, Mr. p. 125
Dwyer, W. T. p. 51

E

Education, Catholic in Pine Bluff p. 116
Education, Parish Religious p. 144
Education, Religious p. 68, 89
Egan, Florence Agnes p. 125
Egan, William p. 125
Eheard, Infant p. 125
Elias, Habib p. 125
Elkins, Iggie, Sr. p. 148
Ellis, Mrs. Mary p. 51
Ellis, Sidney p. 51
Elmer, Theresa p. 51
Embry, Infant p. 125
Embry, Nellie p. 125
Emmett, Miss Bobbie p. 51
Emmett, C. F. p. 51
Emmett, Clifton p. 51
Emmett, Patrick p. 51
Enderby, Mrs. Ethel p. 51
Enderby, Fred p. 51
England, Bishop p. 105
English, E. p. 51
Engright, the Reverend Patrick p. 56
Enright, Rt. Rev. Monsignor Patrick Henry p. 73 (illus.)
Ernst, Albert C. p. 147

177

Ernst, Mr. Albert Charles, Sr. p. 136
Ernst, Mrs. Albert p. 148
Ernst, the Albert, family p. 119
Ernst, the Rev. Albert C., J.C.D. p. 95, 96 (illus.)
Ernst, Annie Bell p. 136
Ernst, family p. 69
Ernst, Louis Gottlieb p. 136
Europe p. 17
Evans, Mrs. Elizabeth p. 51
Evans, W. H. p. 51
Evans, Mr. & Mrs. W. H. p. 69
Evangelization p. 88
"Excursion Through the Slave States" p. 28
Expedition, La Salle's p. 13
Explorers, European p. 13
Explorers, French p. 33
Expressway, Martha Mitchell, north p. 41

F

Families, Catholic p. 16
Families, Early Catholic p. 33
Failla, Harry, family p. 67
Failla, Laura Ferrara p. 118 (illus.)
Fair, Mrs. Frank p. 153, 155
Fairfax, Frances p. 20
Fakouri, Wadie p. 148
Fallin, Edward p. 51
Fallin, Mrs. Mary p. 51
Fannin, Michael p. 125
Faro, Joe p. 125
Farrelly, Adeline p. 20, 103
Farrelly, C. F. p. 20
Farrelly, Nancy p. 20
Fay, Martin p. 126
Featherstonhaugh, G. W. p. 28, 34
Feeley, Charles p. 51
Feeny, John p. 126
Fenwick, Bishop p. 105
Fenwick, J. E. p. 126
Fereio, Ed p. 126
Ferguson, Mrs. Eliza p. 51
Ferguson, Mrs. Edna p. 51
Ferguson, Miss Regina p. 51
Ferguson, Miss Veronica p. 51
Ferguson, Will p. 51
Ferguson, Zachary Howard p. 126
Ferguson, Z. T. p. 126
Fessler, Mrs. Sophia p. 51
Fiest, Joseph p. 126
Finkbeiner, Mary Ann and Paul, Jr. p. 119
Finkbeiner, Mrs. Paul p. 151
Finkbeiner, Mr. & Mrs. Paul p. 69
Finkbeiner, the Paul, family p. 119
Finnegan, Mary Elizabeth p. 103
Finta, Mrs. Anna p. 126

Fitzgerald, Bishop p. 21, 46, 105, 107, 108, 121
Fitzgerald, Bishop Edward p. 116
Fitzgerald, The Most Reverend Edward, D. D. p. 43, 107, 109 (illus.)
Fitzjohn, Infant p. 126
Fitzpatrick, Bernard p. 126
Fletcher, Bishop p. 49, 61, 62, 74, 75, 110, 112, 115, 121, 122
Fletcher, Bishop Albert L. p. 82, 95, 99
Fletcher, Helen Wehr p. 110
Fletcher, His Excellency, Bishop Albert L. p. 82, 117
Fletcher, Monsignor p. 110
Fletcher, The Most Reverend Albert Lewis, D. D. p. 110, 113 (illus.)
Fletcher, Dr. Thomas M. p. 110
"Fletcher's Wilderness" p. 112
Flood, Edward p. 43
Flourney, Chester p. 126
Flynn, Charles Henry p. 126
Flynn, Margurite p. 126
Flynn, Mollie p. 126
Flynn, Mrs. Obe p. 126
Foley, Emily p. 26
Foley, John p. 26
Foley, Michael p. 26, 126
Foley, Missoria p. 26
Foley, Patrick p. 26
Foley, Thomas p. 26
Font, Baptismal p. 67
Fonts, Holy Water p. 60
Ford, Margaret p. 126
Forrester, Patrick p. 126
Foster, Martin p. 51
Foti, Carmela p. 126
Foti, Mrs. Carmela p. 126
Foti, Catherine p. 126
Foti, F. p. 51
Foti, Frank p. 51, 126
Foti, Frank P. p. 51
Foti, Infant p. 126
Foti, Jakey p. 51
Foti, John p. 51, 126
Foti, Joseph p. 51
Foti, Mrs. Mary p. 51
Foti, Mrs. Rosa p. 51
Foti, Mrs. Rosana p. 51
Foti, Stephen, family p. 69
Foti, Vicuizo p. 126
Foundation, The Newman p. 147
Fox, Miss Birdie p. 51
Fox, J. C. p. 51, 126
Fox, J. C., Mrs. p. 126
Fox, Miss Mary p. 51
France p. 14, 35, 84
France, Paris p. 84

Francis, Miss Mary p. 51
Francis, P. J. p. 51
Francis, Mrs. P. J. p. 126
Franey, Miss Anastasia p. 51
Franey, Anthony p. 51
Franey, Miss Catherine p. 51
Franey, Mrs. Catherine p. 51
Franey, Elizabeth Mable p. 126
Franey, family p. 69, 119
Franey, Frank p. 51
Franey, Mrs. James p. 126
Franey, J. F. p. 126
Franey, Mr. J. Frank p. 137, 147
Franey, Toney p. 147
Franey., William p. 51
Franklin, Tim p. 150
Fratesi, Benny J. p. 148
Fratesi, Dan, family p. 119
Frawley, Patrick p. 126
Frazier, L. p. 51
Free Bridge p. 22
French, the p. 13, 14
Frenchman p. 17
Freutel, Miss Josie p. 51
Friday, First p. 151
Friel, D. H. p. 126
Fund, St. Joseph's Educational p. 68
Fund, Theology Scholarship p. 68

G

Gaffney, Father John E. p. 65
Gallagher, Dorothy p. 69
Gallagher, Dr. H. H. p. 51
Gallagher, Mrs. Mary p. 51
Gallagher, Met p. 51
Gallagher, Michael p. 126
Gallagher, Monsignor p. 62, 63, 79, 119
Gallagher, Mrs. p. 69
Gallagher, Patrick p. 126
Gallagher, the Right Rev. Monsignor, Joseph A. p. 61, 78, 79 (illus.)
Galvin, Michael p. 126
Galvin, Patrick p. 126
Gang, Mrs. Frances p. 51
Gang, Frank p. 51
Gang, Peter p. 51
Garney, Anthony p. 51
Garney, Charles p. 51
Garney, George p. 51
Garney, Mrs. Hannah p. 51
Garretty, Thos. p. 126
Garrison, Mrs. Ada p. 51
Gaske, Miss Anna p. 51
Gaske, Felix p. 51
Gaske, Mrs. G. H. p. 148
Gaske, Miss Mary p. 51

Gaske, Mrs. Victoria p. 51
Gaske, W. p. 51
Gazette, Arkansas p. 19
Geary, Mrs. p. 126
Genevay, Albert p. 126
Genevay, Eugene p. 126
Genevay, John p. 51
Genevay, Mrs. Kate p. 126
Genevay, Mrs. K. p. 51
George, Elizabeth Jane p. 26
Georgia, Albany p. 77
Georgia, Port Wentworth p. 112
Georgia, Savannah p. 112
German p. 17
German, Peter p. 40
Germany p. 98
Gibault, Father Pierre p. 14
Gill, Mrs. Elizabeth p. 126
Gill, Infant p. 126
Gill, Miss Lizzie p. 51
Gill, Nathan p. 126
Gill, Rube p. 126
Gilman, Mr. p. 126
Gilman, Mrs. E. J. p. 126
Glogner, Harry Ed p. 127
Gocio, Emily p. 29
Gocio, Joseph p. 29
Gocio, Louis p. 29
Good Shepherd, Sisters of the p. 108
Goodwin, Miss Annie p. 51
Gordy, John p. 118 (illus.)
Gossett, Peter p. 127
Government, United States p. 33
Governor, First Territorial of Arkansas p. 38
Governor, Spanish p. 37
Grace, W. P. p. 138
Gracie, A. E. p. 29
Gracie, J. M. p. 138
Gracie, P. B. p. 29
Gracie, Robert p. 29
Grady, Mrs. Peter p. 127
Grady, Peter T. p. 127
Graham, Edward T. P., Mr. p. 57
Graham, Mrs. Mary p. 51
Grand Prairie Historical Society Bulletin p. 29
Graphic, Pine Bluff p. 137
Graves, Bishop p. 81, 118
Graves, Bishop Lawrence p. 115
Graves, the Most Rev. Lawrence P. p. 64
Graves, the Most Rev. Lawrence Preston, D. D. p. 79, 80 (illus.)
Gravier, Frances p. 37
Gray, Mrs. J. R. p. 158 (illus.)
Green, Annie p. 127
Green, Thomas p. 127
Greenfield, —— p. 20

Greenfield, T. G. p. 20
Greenwood, Mrs. Margaret J. p. 127
Greer, Lottie Ellen p. 127
Grescheck, Mrs. p. 127
Griffin, James p. 51
Griffin, Mrs. p. 127
Griffin, Thomas p. 127
Groce, James C. p. 40
Group, Crucifixion p. 57
Guardian, The p. 48, 108, 118, 151
Guardian, the, Picture Service p. 147
Guignes, Father p. 15
Gunti, Father p. 96
Gunti, Frederick Walter, Mr. p. 95
Gunti, the Rev. Frederick Walter p. 95, 97 (illus.)
Gunti, Mattie Maude Lovelady p. 95
Guynn, Robert Lee p. 127

H

Hacket, Mrs. Eliza p. 127
Haizlip, Mrs. p. 151
Haizlip, Mrs. Millie p. 51
Haley, John p. 127
Hall, Eliza F. p. 140
Hall, Fitzgerald p. 108
Hall, Gallagher p. 62, (illus.) p. 63
Hall, Infant p. 140
Hall, James W. p. 140
Hall, Mrs. L. A. p. 127
Hall, Leonora J. p. 140
Hall, Mattie E. p. 141
Hall, Parish p. 61
Hall, Walter F. p. 141
Hall, Willie E. p. 141
Hallams, Mrs. p. 51
Halpin, Edward p. 127
Halpin, Mrs. p. 127
Hamil, Mrs. Angelina p. 51
Hamilton, Anne p. 43
Hamilton, Henrietta p. 127
Hamilton, Henry p. 127
Hamilton, Dr. J. T. p. 127
Hamilton, Leonore p. 127
Hamilton, Manett Feliciana p. 127
Hamilton, Manette Mary p. 43
Hamilton, Mary Eliza p. 127
Hamilton, Robert Emmett p. 127
Hand, Helping p. 85, 87
Handbook, 1907 p. 50, 51, 52, 53 (illus.)
Hanley, Mr. p. 127
Hanly, Michael , 127
Hannan, Archbishop Phillip M., p. 115
Hardesty, Father Ernest p. 66, 68
Hardin, Ethel p. 141
Hardin, Infant p. 141

Hardin, Maggie p. 141
Harkness, Mrs. Clara p. 51
Harkness, Lee p. 51
Harkness, Leo p. 54
Harkness, Raymond p. 51
Harkness, R.L. p. 55
Hart, Mrs. Elizabeth p. 51
Hart, Harvey p. 51
Hart, Mother Agnes p. 19, 26
Hartnet, Annie p. 127
Hartnet, Infant p. 127
Harvey, Mrs. Amanda p. 51
Harvey, E.B. p. 51
Harvey, James p. 51
Haskins, Rose Sylvester p. 118 (illus.)
Havis, Ferdinand p. 138
Havis, Mrs. Ferdinand p. 127
Hawkins, Joseph B. p. 127
Heissing, James p. 51
Heissing, Mrs. Mary p. 51
Hellet, Cathalena p. 37
Helm, Mrs. Ellen p. 51
Helm, Infant p. 127
Hempstead, "Pictorial History of Arkansas", p. 45
Hemsteager, Joseph Aloysius p. 127
Hemsteager, William Joseph p. 127
Hemsteger, Mrs Mary p. 51
Henberry, —— p. 127
Henderson, Julia Leone p. 127
Henricks, Mrs. M. p. 51
Henton, Catherine L. p. 26
Henton, Lula L. p. 26
Henton, Phillip H. p. 26
Hepburn, Barney F. p. 127
Hessig, Frank p. 127
Hibbard, John p. 20
Hibbard, Martha Ann p. 20
Hibert, "Children of Mr." p. 20
Hibert, Mr. p. 20
Higdon, J.C. p. 127
Higgins, Father p. 74
Higgins, The Reverend Patrick J. p. 56, 74
Higgins, Mrs. Susanna p. 127
Hill, Mrs. Anna p. 51
Hill, Mr. Whatley T. p. 118
Hilton, Thomas H. p. 127
Hinckley, Father E. p. 65
Historic Places, National Register of p. 22
Hoffman, Mrs. Eliza p. 51
Holcombe, —— p. 26
Holcombe, Mrs. B.A. p. 45, 51, 137
Holden, Annie p. 127
Holland, Albert p. 51
Holland, Mrs. Anna p. 51
Holland, Mrs. Annie Wolf p. 127
Holland, James Sell p. 127

Holland, John p. 51
Holland, John J. p. 147
Holland, John Leonard p. 127
Holland, Miss Mary p. 54
Holland, Michael p. 51
Holland, Mike p. 55
Holland, Mrs. Minnie p. 51
Holy See p. 107
Holweck, Rev. F.G. p. 29
Holy Ghost, The Order of The p. 107
Hooper, George p. 51
Hope, Mrs. DeWitt p. 51
Hope, John Herbert p. 127
Hope, Raymond p. 127
Hopkins, Annie J. p. 103
Hopkins, Catherine Ellen p. 127
Hopkins, George Henry p. 127
Hopkins, Mrs. Mary p. 51
Hopkins, Mary Elizabeth Finnegan p. 103
Hopkins, Thomas R. p. 122
Hopkins, Thomas Roland p. 103
Hosler, Mrs. Jane p. 51
Hospital, Charity, New Orleans p. 86
Howard, Ed p. 128
Howard, H. p. 52
Howard, James p. 128
Howard, John p. 128
Howe, Infant p. 128
Hoyler, Mrs. Fred p. 52
Huber, Mrs. Mary p. 52
Hudek, Sister Stephanie, D.C. p. 87, 88 (illus.)
Hudgens, Jane p. 26
Huggard, Mrs. Emma p. 52
Huggard, John p. 128
Huggard, Richard p. 128
Huggard, Thomas p. 52
Hughes, Bishop p. 105
Hughes, Edward p. 128
Hughes, Frank X. p. 147
Hughes, John p. 128
Hulsig, James p. 128
Hume, Mrs. B.H. p. 128
Humphrey, Laura p. 32
Humrichouse, Lucille p. 118 (illus.)
Hunkeler, Bishop Edward J. p. 98

I

Illinois p. 86
Illinois, Effingham p. 136
Illinois, St. Clair County p. 29
Illinois, Western p. 15
Imbeau, Baptiste p. 39
Imbeau, Mary p. 33
Imbrey, Joseph p. 128
Imbrey, Mary p. 128

Independence, Declaration of p. 121
Indian, American p. 13
Indiana p. 86
Indians, Chickasaw p. 21
Indians, Quapaw p. 14, 20, 33, 46
Indians, the p. 14
Infirmary, St. Vincent's—Little Rock p. 74, 82, 110
Institute, Colored Industrial p. 138
Institute, Morris p. 110
Interior, United States Department of the p. 22
Ireland p. 73
Ireland, Athenry, Galway County p. 108
Ireland, Boyle p. 74
Ireland, County Roscommon p. 74
Ireland, Limerick p. 107
Ireland, Navan p. 105
Ish, Mrs. Annie p. 52
Italy p. 57
Italy, Rome p. 76, 80, 98, 108
Ivy, Mrs. Annie p. 52
Ivy—Armfield, family p. 69

J

Jabbur, Eliah p. 52
Jackson, —— p. 52
Jacklin, Father S.F. p. 65
Jackson, John p. 128
Jacob, Joe p. 52
Jacobs, Father David p. 64
James, Mrs. Anna p. 52
James, John p. 52
Janesko, Father Francis J. p. 66
Janin, Father p. 14, 37
Jenkins, Deliah p. 26
Jenkins, Francis N. p. 26
Jenkins, H. p. 26
Jenkins, Dr. J.I. p. 52
Jenkins, Mrs. Lucelia P. p. 68
Jenkins, Mary L. p. 26
Jesuits, of Fort St. Louis, Illinois p. 14
Jesus, Society of p. 98
Johnson, Alla M. p. 128
Johnson, Mrs. Elizabeth p. 52
Johnson, Frank p. 52
Johnson, Henry p. 52
Johnson, Infant p. 128
Johnson, John W. p. 128
Johnson, Mrs. Josephine p. 52
Johnson, Leonard p. 115
Johnson, Miss Lily p. 52
Johnson, Mrs. Lou p. 128
Johnson, Mrs. Matilda p. 52
Johnson, Miss Ruth p. 52
Johnson, William p. 128

Jones, Annie Norris p. 67
Jones, Mrs. Bob p. 128
Jones, Edward p. 52
Jones, George Joseph p. 128
Jones, Infant p. 128
Jones, Richard B. p. 128
Jones, Robert p. 128
Jones, Solon B. p. 121
Jones, Wiley p. 138
Jordelas, Louis p. 36
Josephite Fathers p. 138
Joutel, Lt. p. 14
Joyce, Martin p. 128
Juarez, Felipe p. 128

K

Kalkbrenner, Henry p. 128
Kalkbrenner, Henry and family p. 68
Kane, Michael p. 128
Karlovic, Mrs. J. Edwin p. 117, 148
Karlovic, Mrs. John p. 149
Kavriz, Mrs. p. 128
Keaney, Father Thomas L. p. 65
Keany, Monsignor Thomas L. p. 74
Keefe, Father p. 65
Keeley, Miss Mary p. 52
Keeley, Will p. 52
Keller, Father p. 60, 76
Keller, Father Thomas W. p. 66
Keller, Mrs. Joseph p. 75
Keller, Professor Joseph p. 75
Keller, The Very Reverend Gregory H. p. 59, 75, 76 (illus.)
Kelley, Emma p. 142
Kelly, Birdie p. 128
Kelly, Daniel p. 128
Kelly, Dennis p. 141
Kelly, Mrs. Mary p. 128
Kelly, Myrtle p. 128
Kembramer, Frank Thomas p. 128
Kenna, Thomas p. 128
Kennedy, John p. 52
Kennedy, Mrs. John p. 52
Kennedy, Jon p. 38
Kentucky, Bardstown p. 104
Kentucky, Crab Orchard Springs p. 103
Kentucky, Harrodsburg p. 37
Kentucky, Lebanon p. 108
Kentucky, Munfordsville, Hart County p. 108
Kentucky, Nazareth p. 103, l04
Kerwin, Catherine p. 128
Kerwin, Mrs. Carolina p. 52
Kerwin, Dan, Sr. p. 128
Kerwin, Daniel p. 128
Kerwin, Edwin J. p. 147

Kerwin, E.J. p. 52
Kerwin, Mrs. Ellen p. 52
Kerwin, John p. 52
Kerwin, John J. p. 55
Kerwin, Mrs. Margaret p. 52
Kessel, Mr. and Mrs. Louis J. p. 69
Kettler, Father John J. p. 66
Kidd, Mrs. Vernon p. 92
Kilday, Martin p. 128
Kilpatrick, Father F.J. p. 65
Kilroy, Anna Emma p. 128
King, Carmen p. 91
King, Curtis p. 91
King, F.P. p. 52
King, Mrs. F.P. p. 52
King, Frank P. p. 70
King, Frank Velvin (Buddy) p. 90 (illus.), 91
King, Harry E. p. 147
King, Mrs. Harry p. 118
King, Harry E., family p. 119
King, Infant p. 128
King, Judy p. 91
King, Kevin p. 91
King, William H. p. 148
Kinney, John p. 129
Kirchgraber, family p. 69
Kirchgraber, John p. 54
Kleinschmidt, Sister Maria, D.C. p. 88, 89 (illus.), 145
Knight, Grand p. 136
Knights, Grand p. 147
Knoeber, Father Joe p. 66
Kohlbrenner, Henry p. 52
Kohlbrenner, Louis p. 52
Kohlbrenner, Mrs. Mary p. 52
Kohlbrenner, Miss Rose p. 52
Koshel, Brynn p. 150
Koschel, Mrs. Leroy p. 144 (illus.), 145
Koster, J. p. 52
Koury, Joe p. 52
Kraeszig, Mr. and Mrs. Fred p. 103
Kraeszig, Leona p. 103
Kramer, Paul p. 129
Kuhner, Felix p. 52
Kuhner, Mary p. 52

L

Lacardi, Infant p. 129
Lacardi, Minnie p. 129
Lamonica, Ada p. 52
Lamonica, Bernard p. 52
Lamonica, Miss Fannie p. 52
Lamonica, Lee p. 52
Lamonica, Mrs. Mary p. 52
Lamonica, Miss Rose p. 52
Lampert, Ben p. 52

Lampert, Mrs. Catherine p. 52
Lampert, Fred p. 52
Lampert, Infant p. 129
Lampert, John Edward p. 129
Lampert, Lennie p. 129
Lampert, Mrs. Louisa p. 52
Lamps, Sanctuary p. 57
Land, Amanda Jane p. 74
Land, Congress p. 18
Language, Indian p. 35
La Salle p. 33
Latin p. 35
Laude, Joseph p. 129
Lauders, Mrs. Amanda p. 129
Laughlin, Father Joseph J. p. 65
Laughran, Reverend Francis p. 43, 71
Laux, Elizabeth p. 82
Law, Canon p. 68
Laxton, Mrs. Jennie p. 52
Lay People, the Apostolate of p. 68
Lazzarani, Natalina p. 52
Leas, Augusta Fischer p. 137
Leas, Mr. Leslie E. p. 137
Leas, Russell D. p. 137
Lee, B. p. 19
Lee, F. p. 19
Lehman, A. p. 52
Lehman, Alford p. 129
Lehman, George p. 129
Lehman, Miss Josephine p. 52
Lehman, Mrs. Mary p. 52
Lehnert, Miss Annie p. 52
Lehnert, Mrs. Gussie p. 52
Lehnert, John p. 52, 129
Leidinger, Louis p. 129
Leland, Annie (or Ida) p. 129
Lemmans, Mrs. Ellen p. 129
Leo VII, Pope p. 15
Leo, Sister Mary, S.C.N. p. 67
Leonard, Balf (?), p. 129
Leonard, John Edmund p. 129
Leonard, John J. p. 129
LeSieur, Father David p. 68
LeSieur, Mr. and Mrs. Charles p. 96
LeSieur, Mrs. Charles p. 118
LeSieur, The Reverend Charles David p. 96, 98 (illus.)
Lewis, Mrs. Charles p. 52
Liberty, D. p. 52
Library, Jefferson County Public p. 48
Lihof, (?), J. p. 129
Limbaugh, James p. 52
Lindsey, John Andrew p. 129
Lines, Apache Van, Inc. p. 91
List, Miss Amalie
Lites Studio p. 83
Little Rock p. 18, 21
Little Rock, Bishop of p. 56, 110, 112

Little Rock, Diocese of p. 7, 15, 20, 62, 68, 74, 91, 105, 107, 117
Little Rock, Fifth Bishop of p. 112
Little Rock, First Bishop of p. 105
Little Rock, Fourth Bishop of p. 110
Little Rock, Second Bishop of p. 107
Little Rock, See of p. 108
Little Rock, Third Bishop of p. 108
Little Rock, Vice—General, Diocese of p. 72
Locardi, John p. 52
Locardi, Joseph p. 52
Locardi, Peter p. 52
Locardi, Pio p. 52
Locardi, Mrs. Theresa p. 52
Locardi, Victor p. 52
Lomonico, Mary p. 129
Loretto, Sisters of p. 19, 29
Loring, Ellar p. 129
Louisiana p. 14, 16, 35, 86, 89
Louisiana, Diocese of p. 15
Louisiana, New Orleans p. 74, 87, 136, 145
Louisiana, Shreveport p. 95
Lovelady, Mrs. Mary p. 52
Lovelady, Maude p. 129
Lovejoy, Mrs. George p. 52
Lubry, Infant p. 129
Lucas, James p. 15
Lucey, Father p. 21, 46, 49, 72
Lucey, Monsignor p. 41, 49, 56, 57, 121
Lucey, Monsignor J.M. p. 122
Lucey, Monsignor John M. p. 116, 120, 150
Lucey, The Reverend John M. p. 46
Lucey, The Right Reverend John M. p. 67
Lucey, Right Reverend J.M. p. 54
Lucey, The Right Reverend Monsignor John M. p. 138
Lucey, Right Reverend Monsignor, V.G. p. 71, 72 (illus.)
Lucke, —— p. 129
Lucke, A.B. p. 129
Luneau, Father Harold p. 66
Luneau, Mrs. M.D. p. 158 (illus.)
Luperini, Angelo p. 52
Lupo, Dave p. 148
Lynch, Mrs. Catherine p. 52
Lynch, Charlotte p. 103
Lynch, Donald B., Mr. p. 92 (illus.), 103, 148
Lynch, Mary p. 103
Lynch, Mrs. p. 92
Lynch, Owen p. 129
Lynch, Patrick p. 129
Lynch, Sister Donald Mary, R.S.M. p. 103

Mc

McBride, Bernard C. p. 129
McCann, Amand p. 20

McCann, F. p. 20
McCann, Teresia p. 20
McCarthy, Mrs. Catherine p. 52
McCarthy, C.F. p. 52
McCarthy, Father Kevin p. 66
McCarthy, John p. 129
McCauley, Father R.J. p. 65
McCauley, Kathleen Rose p. 98
McClosky, The Most Reverend John p. 105
McConnell, Infant p. 129
McCormack, Bob p. 77
McCormick, John p. 129
McCoy, Father Charles B. p. 65
McCoy, Jim p. 52
McCrane, John p. 129
McDermott, John C. p. 129
McDermott, Mrs. John C. p. 129
McDonald, Andrew J., Bishop of Little Rock p. 7
McDonald, Bishop p. 64, 112, 118
McDonald, Bishop Andrew J. p. 64, 95, 96, 137
McDonald, His Excellency, Bishop p. 112
McDonald, His Excellency, Bishop Andrew J. p. 6 (illus.), 7, 91
McDonald, Right Reverend Monsignor Andrew J. p. 112
McDonald, The Most Reverend Andrew J., D.D. p. 112, 114 (illus.)
McDonald, The Very Reverend Monsignor Andrew J. p. 112
McEvoy, John p. 129
McEwen, James A. p. 148
McGaughey, Joseph p. 52
McGaughey, Mrs. Stella p. 52
McGeorge, Mrs. Wallace p. 153
McGhee, Michael p. 129
McGinnis, —— p. 129
McGinnis, Father Charles p. 65
McGinnis, Father N. Charles p. 61
McGlenn, —— p. 52
McGlynn, Annie p. 129
McGlynn, Catherine p. 129
McGlynn, Mrs. Catherine p. 130
McGlynn, Infant p. 130
McGlynn, James p. 130
McGlynn, Katie p. 130
McGlynn, Mary Ann p. 130
McGlynn, Mathew p. 130
McGlynn, Mattie p. 130
McGlynn, Patrick p. 130
McGlynn, Peter p. 130
McGowan, Father p. 105
McGrath, Mrs. R.F. p. 155, 149
McGregor, Andrew p. 130
McGuire, J. p. 20
McGuire, Miss p. 20
McKay, Robert p. 16

McKenzie, O.E. p. 142
McKeown, Rev. Thomas p. 15
McKevit, John P. p. 130
McKnight, Allie May p. 130
McKnight, James p. 52, 130
McKnight, John p. 52
McKnight, Thomas p. 52
McLane, Isaac p. 16
McLaughlin, Father Paul p. 66
McMahan, John p. 130
McManus, Infant p. 130
McNally, Adele Carroll p. 130
McNally, Charles p. 130
McNally, John p. 130
McNally, Mary p. 130
McNeal, Henry p. 27
McNulty, A. p. 52
McNulty, Mrs. Salina p. 52
McNulty, Thomas p. 130
McQueeny, William p. 130
McTierney, Miss Nellie p. 52
McTierney, Peter p. 52

M

Maguire, Father V.E. p. 66
Maguire, Thomas p. 130
Mahar, Mrs. Johannah p. 52
Mahar, John T. p. 130
Mahar, William p. 130
Maher, Fred I. p. 148
Maher, Fred I., family p. 69
Maher, Mrs. Johanna p. 130
Maher, Maas, family p. 69
Maiani, Adams; p. 52
Malaney, John p. 52
Malfitti, Lorenzo p. 130
Malley, D.P. p. 130
Malley, Infant p. 130
Malley, Mary Frances p. 130
Malone, Father Bernard p. 66
Malone, Thomas p. 130
Malpose, James p. 20
Malpose, John p. 20
Mancini, Father James E. p. 66
Maney, Mrs. p. 130
Manley, Patrick p. 130
Many, Martin p. 130
Manzer, Mrs. p. 52
Mara, Mrs. M.L. p. 52
Mara, Will p. 52
Mara, William J. p. 147
Marble, Carrara p. 57, 63
Marino, Neddo p. 52
Marino, Neddo J. p. 148
Markey, Sister Catherine, M.H.S. p. 11
Marlo, Mrs. C.F. p. 153 (illus.)

Marquette, Father Jacques p. 13
Marquette, Père. the Explorations of, p. 12 (illus.)
Marshall, J.L. p. 52
Martin, Mrs. Carl p. 157 (illus.)
Martin, Father John p. 16
Mary, Blessed Virgin p. 57
Mary, The Legion of p. 153
Maryland, Archbishop of Primatial See of Baltimore p. 121
Maryland, Baltimore p. 112
Maryland, Carroll family of p. 121
Maryland, Emmitsburg p. 107
Mason, Ellen p. 130
Mass of Christian Burial p. 76
Mass, Holy Sacrifice of The p. 59, 60
Mass, Pontifical p. 105
Mass, Solemn Requiem Funeral p. 74
Massachusetts, Boston p. 57, 105, 138
Massanelli, Infant p. 130
Massanelli, Mr. Tim p. 58, 93 (illus.), 148
Mattmiller, Mrs. Lulu p. 52
Matz, Barbara Josephine p. 130
Matz, Charles p. 52
Matz, Mrs. Elizabeth p. 52
Matz, family p. 69
Matz, Miss Hilda p. 151, 118
Matz, John p. 52
Matz, Nick p. 52
Matz, Mrs. Rosa p. 52
Matz, Miss Stella p. 52
Maulding, John p. 120
Maxwell, David p. 20
Mayer, Mrs. Amalia p. 52
Mayer, Charles. p. 52
Mayer, Miss Ida p. 52, 130
Mayer, Joseph p. 52
Mayer, Miss Lilly p. 52
Mayer, Mrs. Rosa p. 52
Mayfield, Mattie p. 26
Mayhan, Mrs. Paul p. 144 (illus.), 145
Membre, Father Zanobius p. 14
Men, Dioceson Council of Catholic p. 83
Mercy, Religious Sisters of p. 103, 110
Mercy, Sisters of p. 107
Merle, Annie p. 69
Merle, William F. p. 69
Merlo, James p. 52
Merlo, John p. 52
Merlo, John, family p. 69
Merlo, Miss Mary p. 52
Merlo, Mrs. Mary p. 52
Merlo, Pio p. 52
Merrick, Mrs. p. 52
Merrill, Mrs. Albina p. 52
Merrill, Joe p. 52
Meurin, Father p. 15
Meyer, Mrs. Gabe p. 68

Meyer, family p. 68
Meyer, John p. 130
Meyer, William p. 130
Mexico, Gulf of p. 13
"M.C." p. 32
Michael, Eliah p. 52
Michael, Mrs. Mary p. 52
Michalotti, Eugene p. 52
Michelotti, Gabriel p. 52
Michelotti, Joseph p. 52
Michelotti, Mrs. Naterlina p. 52
Michelotti, Pierre p. 52
Michellotte, Lawrence p. 130
Miller, Mrs. Albertina p. 52
Miller, Mrs. Don p. 149
Miller, Henry W. p. 115
Miller, James p. 38
Miller, John p. 130
Miller, Nathaniel p. 52
Miller, Mrs. Theresa p. 52
Miller, William p. 52
Minnesota, Minneapolis p. 92
Minnesota, Winona p. 88
Ministry, Parish p. 89
Ministry, Youth p. 68
Minor, Order of Friars p. 97
Minoret, family p. 69
Mission, Congregation of The, Chapter 1, #18 (footnote), p. 159
Mission, Indian p. 14
Mission, St. Peter's p. 138
Missionaries p. 13
Missionaries, Lazarist p. 21
Missionary, Recollect p. 14
Mississippi, Jackson p. 96
Mississippi, the p. 15
Missouri p. 15, 88
Missouri, Barry County p. 35
Missouri, Christian County p. 35
Missouri, Douglas County .p. 35
Missouri, Kansas City p. 85
Missouri, New Madrid p. 14
Missouri, Ozark County p. 35
Missouri, Perry County p. 107
Missouri, Perry County, Apple Creek p. 17
Missouri, Perryville p. 86
Missouri, Springfield p. 93
Missouri, St. Louis p. 84, 86, 92, 107
Missouri, Stone County p. 35
Missouri, Taney County p. 35
Mitchell, Elizabeth Piere p. 20
Mitchell, Mrs. Ellen p. 151
Mitchell, Mrs. Fanny p. 26
Mitchell, Frank p. 26
Mitchell, Frank B. p. 147
Mitchell, J.C. p. 26
Mitchell, J.M. p. 26
Mitchell, John p. 26, 130

185

Mitchell, John B., Jr. p. 26
Mitchell, John B., Sr. p. 26
Mitchell, Louis p. 26
Mitchell, Peter p. 26
Mitchell, Piere p. 20
Mitchell, Mrs. Wiley p. 148
Mitchell, Mrs. Z. F. p. 151
Mitosinka, John p. 143
Moellers, John p. 150
Moellers, Robert p. 149, 150
Moellers, Mr. Robert L. p. 155
Monestra, Samuel p. 52
Monestra, Toney p. 52
Montaique, Miss Augusta p. 52
Montaique, C.H. p. 52
Montgomery, Robert Alexander p. 130
Mooney, Augustine p. 52
Mooney, Father Edward L. p. 66
Mooney, H.A. p. 52
Mooney, J. Pelton p. 148
Mooney, Joseph p. 52
Mooney, Mrs. Mary p. 52
Mooney, Thomas p. 52
Mooney, William p. 52
Moore, Adeline Farrelly p. 103
Moore, C.F. p. 52, 121
Moore, Mrs. C.F. p. 22
Moore, Charles F. p. 147
Moore, Fannie p. 103
Moore, Mrs. James p. 92
Moore, James Harlan p. 103
Moore, Joseph S. p. 29
Moore, Mrs. Julia S. p. 29
Moore, Rose p. 103
Moore, Thomas p. 131
Mora, Michael p. 131
Moran, Miss Agnes p. 148
Moran, William p. 131
Moreau, Robert p. 52
Morris, Bishop p. 22, 61, 72, 75, 108, 110
Morris, Bishop John B. p. 78, 80
Morris, Bishop, Third of Little Rock p. 56
Morris, His Excellency, John B. p. 59
Morris, John p. 108
Morris, John B., Bishop of Little Rock p. 74
Morris, M.G. p. 45
Morris, M.J. p. 52
Morris, The Most Reverend John Baptist, D.D. p. 108, 111 (illus.)
Morris, The Right Reverend John B. p. 74
Morris, Right Reverend Monsignor John Baptist p. 108
Morris, The Very Reverend Bishop John B. p. 73
Morrow, Mrs. A. p. 52
Morrow, G.W. p. 52
Morrow, Morris p. 131
Moser, Joseph Charles p. 131

Moser, Frank Adam p. 131
Moser, Miss Jennie p. 52
Moser, Joseph p. 52
Moser, Miss Lena p. 52
Moser, Miss Lizzie p. 52
Moser, Miss Neddie p. 52
Moser, Oswald p. 52
Moser, Mrs. Theresa p. 52
Motherhouse—Paris p. 84
Mount St. Mary's, Emmitsburg, Maryland p. 107
Mount St. Mary's of the West, Cincinnati, Ohio p. 107
Mountain, Miss Grace p. 52
Mountain, Miss Mary p. 52
Mountain, Mrs. Sarah Roundtree p. 131
Mulligan, Father John p. 65
Mulligan, Thomas p. 131
Murphy, Mrs. Barbara p. 52
Murphy, Carter p. 52
Murphy, Catherine Beatrice p. 131
Murphy, Fanny p. 29
Murphy, Father J.F. p. 65
Murphy, Frances p. 131
Murphy, Francis D. p. 29
Murphy, James p. 29
Murphy, John p. 131
Murphy, John P. p. 131
Murphy, J.P. p. 45
Murphy, Matthew p. 29
Murphy, Patrick p. 131
Murphy, Robert Ernest Lee p. 131
Murphy, Solon Washington p. 131
Murphy, Walter C. p. 29
Murr, Max p. 131
Murray, Charles, p. 131
Murray, Hugh p. 26
Murray, James p. 131
Murray, Mrs. Peter p. 131
Murtaugh, John p. 131
Music, Church p. 68
Mustacchia, Antonio p. 52
Mustacchia, Miss Anna p. 52
Mustacchia, Frank p. 52
Mustacchia, John p. 52
Mustacchia, Joseph p. 52
Mustacchia, Mrs. Lulu p. 52
Mustacchia, Maggie Laurine p. 131
Mustacchia, Mrs. Mary p. 52
Mustacchia, Mary Lena p. 131
Mustacchia, Nick p. 52
Mustacchia, Paschal p. 52, 131
Mustacchia, Mrs. Pearl p. 52
Mustacchia, Peter p. 52
Myers, D.J. p. 52

N

Nave, East, old St. Joseph's p. 46
Nacke, Father p. 65
Navan, Diocesan Seminary of p. 105
Navigator, Faithful p. 136
Nazareth, The Sisters of Charity of p. 49, 62, 103, 104, 116, 117, 138
Neal, Joe Davis p. 32
Nebraska, Diocese of Lincoln p. 85
Nebraska, Omaha p. 98
Neece, Mrs. Charles Max p. 148
"Nellie" p. 110
Neuzil, Father Procipino p. 65
New Gascony p. 18, 29, 33, 38
New Gascony, St. Peter's p. 28
New Orleans p. 19, 35
New Orleans, See of p. 15
New York, Troy p. 71
Noble, Cathalena Hellet p. 37
Noble, Elizabeth Carle p. 37
Noble, Frances Gravier p. 37
Noble, Jacoba p. 37
Noble, John p. 37
Noble, Juan p. 37
Noble, Mackerly Carola p. 37
Noble, Marco p. 37
Noble Lake, Jefferson Co., Ark. p. 142
Norris, A.M. p. 151
Norris, Mrs. A.M. p. 52, 150
Norton, Father p. 65
Notrebene, Frederick p. 15, 35

O

Oaks, Infant p. 131
Oaks, J.H. p. 131
Oaks, Mrs. Nellie p. 52
Oaks, Ruby p. 131
O'Brian, James D. p. 131
O'Brien, Mrs. J. p. 52
O'Brien, Johanna p. 131
O'Brien, Sister Silvia p. 116
O'Connell, Emily p. 131
O'Connell, Mrs. Emma p. 53
O'Connell, Emma May p. 131
O'Connell, John p. 52
O'Connell, Miss Lena p. 53
O'Connell, Miss Leicester p. 53
O'Connell, Patrick p. 27
Odin, Father p. 18
Odin, Father John p. 16
O'Donnell, Bridget p. 81
O'Donnell, Father p. 64, 82
O'Donnell, Father John Francis p. 81
O'Donnell, Henry p. 81
O'Donnell, Peter p. 131
O'Donnell, The Reverend John Francis p. 64, 81 (illus.)
Officialis of the Diocese of Savannah p. 112
Ohio, Cincinnati p. 87, 107
Ohio, Columbus p. 107
O'Keefe, May p. 118
O'Keiff, Anthony p. 131
O'Keiff, Mrs. B. p. 131
O'Keiff, Mrs. Elizabeth p. 53
O'Keiff, Jack p. 53
O'Keiff, James Charles Joseph p. 131
O'Keiff, Mrs. Scottie p. 53
O'Leary, Dennis p. 131
O'Leary, John p. 131
O'Leary, Odellia p. 131
Olson, Eli p. 131
Olson, Mrs. John p. 131
Olympics, Special p. 146, 147
O'Mark, (?), Infants, (twins) p. 131
Omcirck, Edwin p. 131
Omcirck, Infant p. 131
Omcirck, Infants (twins) p. 131
Omcirck, Joseph p. 131
O'Neil, Charlie p. 53
O'Neil, Father Lawrence p. 65
O'Neil, Frank Joseph p. 131
O'Neil, Miss Irene p. 53
O'Neil, John p. 53
O'Neil, Mrs. Louisa p. 53
O'Neil, Maggie p. 131
O'Neil, Martin p. 53
O'Neil, Mrs. Nellie p. 53
Order, Franciscan p. 97
Order of Friars Minor p. 97
Orders, Religious p. 107
Organists, St. Joseph's p. 158 (illus.)
Organization, Catholic Youth p. 149 (illus.)
Organizations, Church p. 146
Organization, Senior Catholic Youth p. 82
Ormond, Mrs. Annie p. 132
Ormond, John p. 132
Ormond, John George p. 132
Ormond, Thomas p. 132
Ormsis, Joseph p. 53
Ormsis, Mrs. Josephine p. 53
"Oro Ecclesia Et Pontifice" p. 137
Orphanage, St. Joseph's p. 82, 108, 147
O'Rourke, Mrs. p. 131
O'Rourke, William p. 132
O'Sullivan, Florence p. 132
O'Sullivan, Florence, Jr. p. 132
O'Sullivan, Mary Ellen p. 132
O'Sullivan, Mrs. Mary Florence p. 132
Owens, J.W. p. 138

P

Padres, Missionary p. 33
Paechtel, Miss Catherine p. 53
Paechtel, Miss Lena p. 53
Pallo, Father Joseph p. 66
Palmer, Tom p. 132
Palmer, Willie p. 132
Parenti, Infant p. 132
Parish, Our Lady of Lourdes, Port Wentworth, Ga. p. 112
Parish, St. Joseph's p. 9, 11, 37, 64, 151
Parish, St. Mary's p. 37
Parishes, Arkansas p. 68
Parker, Charles p. 53
Parker, Francis p. 53
Parker, Joseph p. 53
Parker, Mrs. Mary p. 53
Parlis, Mrs. Mary p. 53
Patterson, Mrs. Emily p. 53
Patterson, Mrs. E.M. p. 132
Patterson, Emilie M. p. 69
Pattillo, Mrs. Stuart p. 151
Patton, Elnora p. 27
Patton, Mary C. p. 27
Paul VI, Pope p. 64, 81, 112
Paulite, Mrs. p. 20
Paull, Mrs. A. p. 53
Payne, Mrs. Caroline p. 53
Payne, family p. 68
Pendleton, Dr. P.H. p. 132
Pendleton, Dr. Plesant H. p. 103
Pendleton, Mrs. P.H. p. 151
Pendleton, Sister Adelaide, S.C.N. p. 103
Pennsylvania, Philadelphia p. 62, 64, 78, 81
Perry, Jack p. 132
Perry, Mrs. Jack p. 132
Pertuis, Elizabeth p. 19
Pertuis, John p. 15
Pertuis, M. p. 19
Pertuis, Manuel p. 15
Peter, Mrs. p. 27
Peterson, Mrs. A. p. 53
Petit Rocher p. 18
Petrus, Dan p. 147 (illus.), 148
Petrus, Mrs. Daniel J. p. 149
Phelan, Father p. 105
Phelps, Miss Mary p. 53
Phelps, Mrs. Mary p. 53
Phelps, Miss Sadie p. 53
Philpot, Mrs. C.E. p. 132
Picchi, Miss Elizabeth p. 53
Picchi, Peter p. 53
Pichi, Infant p. 132
Picket, Mrs. Agnes p. 53
Picket, Infant p. 132
Picket, Miss Ruth p. 53

Pickett, George p. 132
"Pilot, The" p. 138
Pincard, William M. p. 41
Pine Bluff p. 16, 18, 21, 22, 28, 31, 32, 34, 37, 39, 40, 43, 49, 56, 57, 64
Pine Bluff, Catholic Parish in p. 44
Pine Bluff, Kiwanis Club of p. 91
Pine Bluff, Lake p. 41
Pine Bluff, St. Joseph's p. 7, 73
Pine Bluff, Town of p. 41
Pinkney, Mrs. Anna p. 53
Pinkney, Pembroke p. 53
Pinot, Antoine p. 15
Pinot, Amelia A. p. 29
Pinot, Augustin p. 15
Pinot, Emelia E. p. 29
Pius X Boarding Home for Children p. 85
Pius X, Pope p. 72
Pius XII, Pope p. 110
Placy, Louis p. 15
Plum Bayou p. 20
Plum Bayou, St. Mary's p. 22
Poff, Oscar Thomas p. 132
Point, Boyd's p. 22
Pompili, Cardinal p. 76
Pope, Governor John p. 21
Popes
  Pope Leo VII p. 15
  Pope Paul VI p. 64, 81, 112
  Pope Pius X p. 72
  Pope Pius XII p. 110
Pordini, Domenico p. 132
Portis, Charles B., Rev. p. 132
Portis, James p. 132
Portis, John p. 132
Portis, Mrs. Mary p. 67
Portis, Mrs. p. 151
Post, Arkansas p. 7, 13, 14, 15, 20, 33, 35, 137
Post, Arkansas, Commandant of p. 37
Post, Illinois p. 14
Postmaster p. 38
Postmaster, first p. 39
Post, the p. 18
Posts p. 13
Powers, Mrs. p. 53
Prelate, Domestic p. 72, 79, 112
Priest, Franciscan p. 14
Priest, Sulpitian p. 14
Priests, French p. 20
Priests, Irish p. 20
Priests, Jesuit
Price, Mrs. Benjamin p. 53
Primeau, Mrs. p. 132
Program, Parish Religious Education p. 145
Programs, Coordinator for Holy Year p. 64, 82
Prost, The Most Reverend Jude, O.F.M.

188

Protestant p. 18
Province, Sacred Heart p. 97
Provincial Council, Second of Baltimore p. 105
Prye, Mary E. p. 132
Puddephatt, Mrs. William p. 151, 153
Purcell, Archbishop J.B. p. 107
Pyrenees, lower p. 28

Q

Quapaw p. 20
Quapaws p. 35
Quartier, The Most Reverend William p. 105
Quinn, Father D.A. p. 105

R

Ragan, Mrs. Mattie p. 151
Rail, Communion p. 57
Railroad, Cotton Belt p. 136
Railroad, Illinois Central p. 136
Raimondi, Archbishop Luigi p. 115
Rawls, Mrs. Rosa p. 132
Rebeccah, Alyhouse p. 53
Rebeccah, Miss Corinne p. 53
Rebeccah, Gasparo p. 53
Rebeccah, George p. 53
Rebeccah, Mrs. Josephine p. 53
Rebeccah, Miss Mary p. 53
Reconstruction p. 107
Records, Arkansas County p. 35
Records, Cemetery, St. Mary's p. 16, 22, 24
Records, Cemetery, St. Peter's, New Gascony p. 29, 30
Records, Diocesan p. 41
Records, French p. 24
Records, Interment, St. Joseph's, 1840–1913 p. 122–135
Rectory, St. Patrick's, North Little Rock p. 81
Red Bluff p. 28
Redding, Edward p. 53
Redding, Infant p. 132
Redelman, Gil p. 148
Reder, Fred p. 53
Redfield p. 28
Redmann, Adeline p. 132
Redmond, Infant p. 132
Reeder, Miss p. 20
Reeder, Thomas p. 20
Regent, State, Ark. State Court of Catholic Daughters p. 148
Regime, Spanish p. 14
Register, National p. 22
Reh, The Most Reverend Francis F., J.C.D. p. 96
Reidenger, Louis C. p. 132

Relic p. 57
Remond, Mrs. Mary p. 53
Rent, pew receipt p. 45 (illus.)
Report, Annual 1911, p. 54, 55 (illus.)
Representatives, Arkansas House of p. 93
Reservation, Quapaw p. 21
Reserve, Bonne p. 33
Reserve, Valliere p. 31
Reyer, Mrs. Henry p. 148
Reyer, Mr. and Mrs. H.E. p. 69
Reynolds, Mrs. Carolina p. 53
Reynolds, Miss Ellen p. 53
Reynolds, Father Thomas P. p. 65
Reynolds, G.G. p. 132
Reynolds, Henry p. 53
Reynolds, John p. 132
Reynolds, Katie p. 132
Richmond, Bertha p. 142
Richmond, Charles H. p. 142
Richmond, Corine p. 142
Rickels, Beth Ross p. 97
Rickels, Charles p.97
Rickels, Father p. 97
Rickels, The Reverend Raymond, O.F.M. p. 97, 99 (illus.)
Rides, Mrs. Anna p. 132
Riedmueller, Elizabeth Laux p. 82
Riedmueller, Father p. 64, 82, 83
Riedmueller, Father Leo p. 11
Riedmueller, George W. p. 82
Riedmueller, The Reverend Leo A. p. 9, 64
Riedmueller, The Very Reverend Leo Anthony, V.F. p. 8 (illus.), 82, 83 (illus.), 154 (illus.)
Rifles, Fort Smith p. 71
Rigney, Huldah p. 19
Rigney, Isabelle p. 19
Rigney, W. p. 19
Rike, family p. 69
Riley, Mrs. p. 53
Rivers
  Arkansas River p. 7, 13, 15, 16, 20, 22, 33
  Mississippi River p. 13, 14
  Red River p. 14
Road, Altheimer—Reydel p. 28
Roane, Frances p. 19
Roane, Mary p. 19
Roane, Judge Samuel C. p. 19
Roberts, Mrs. p. 53
Rocher, Marie p. 132
Rocher, Petit p. 18
Rodgers, Infant p. 132
Rodgers, Mrs. Curtis p. 117, 118
Roney, John p. 132
Rooney, Thomas p. 132
Rosati, Bishop p. 16, 17, 18, 19, 28
Rosati, Joseph, Bishop of St. Louis p. 41
"Rosati, the Arkansas Mission Under" p. 29

Rosati, The Most Reverend John p. 15
Rosati, The Reverend John, C.M. p. 15
Rose, John, family p. 119
Rose, Joseph p. 132
Ross, Beth p. 97
Ross, Mary p. 132
Rosser, Eli p. 132
Rottet, Mrs. Lillian p. 53
Rottet, R.B. p. 53
Royston, Francis p. 53
Rucker. Caryl Colquitt p. 118 (illus.)
Rucker, Mrs. Steve p. 149
Rucker, Mrs. W.A. p. 118
Rucker, W.L., family p. 119
Rudder, Mrs. Mary p. 133
Ruggeri, Augusto p. 133
Ruggeri, Primo, family p. 68, 119
Russell, —— p. 53
Ryan, James p. 133

S

Saconi, Eddie C. p. 133
Saconi, Joseph p. 133
Sacconi, Mrs. p. 133
Sacraments, The p. 18
Saint Genevieve p. 15
Saint Vincent de Paul, The Daughters of Charity of p. 84
Samos, Titular Bishop of p. 110
Saracen p. 20, 21, 46
Saracen, Chief of the Quapaws p. 133
Sarasen p. 121
Sarazin, Cadet Francois p. 20
Satterwhite, Mrs. p. 133
Saulnier p. 17
Saulnier, Father p. 17, 18
Saulnier, Father Edmund p. 16
Saulnier, Mr. p. 17
Saunders, Father Leo p. 65
Sauter, Edward J. p. 147
Savannah, Diocese of p. 112
Savannah, Vicar General for the Diocese of p. 112
Savary, D. p. 133
Scanlen, family p. 69
Schaep, George John Peter p. 133
Schlater, Infant p. 133
Schnable, Annie p. 133
Schneider, Mrs. Nannie p. 133
Schlemer, Mrs. Carolina p. 53
Schlemer, John p. 53
Schools
   Catholic High, Little Rock p. 80, 82
   Catholic High School p. 96, 82, 110
   Catholic School p. 19
   Creighton Preparatory School p. 98
   Dial Junior High School p. 95
   Epiphany School p. 78
   Mount Carmel School p. 78
   Northeast Catholic High School, Philadelphia, Pa. p. 82
   Pine Bluff Catholic School p. 116, 119
   Pine Bluff High School p. 95
   Roman Catholic High School p. 78
   Sacred Heart School, Morrilton, Ark., p. 82, 98
   St. Andrew's Cathedral School p. 75
   St. Edward's Parochial School p. 79, 80
   St. Edward's, Texarkana p. 96
   St. James Parochial School, San Francisco p. 78
   St. Joseph's Catholic School p. 63, 117
   St. Joseph's School p. 116, 118
   St. Mary's Dominican High School p. 145
   St. Peter's School p. 118
   Whitehall High School p. 97
Schrader, Mrs. Annie p. 53
Schrader, Ernest p. 53
Scott, D. E. p. 133
Scott, Father p. 65
Scott, Miss p. 53
Scouts, Boy p. 146
Scull p. 29
Scull, Ann Maria p. 20
Scull, Ben p. 53
Scull, Ben H. p. 98
Scull, Miss Blanche p. 53
Scull, Cordelia Rabron p. 44
Scull, Mrs. Ed p. 53
Scull, family p. 41
Scull, Father p. 98
Scull, F. Knox p. 147
Scull, Frances p. 20, 133
Scull, Frederick p. 43
Scull, Hewes p. 15, 16, 37, 133, 137
Scull, James p. 20, 30, 36, 37, 38, 121
Scull, James Hewes p. 133
Scull, Mrs. J.H. p. 133
Scull, J. Hewes p. 45
Scull, James Knox p. 133
Scull, The Reverend James P., S.J. p. 97, 100 (illus.)
Scull, John C. Jones p. 30
Scull, Kathleen Rose McCauley p. 98
Scull, Knox p. 53
Scull, Louisa p. 30
Scull, Mrs. L.P. p. 45, 53
Scull, Mrs. Louisiana Philipena p. 133, 137
Scull, Mary Louisa p. 30
Scull, Manette Vaugine p. 36, 38
Scull, Mary p. 133
Scull, Nicholas p. 133
Scull, Roberta A. p. 133

Scull, Mrs. Sadie p. 53
Scull, Mr. William B. p. 44
Scull, William Frederick p. 133
Seagram, Joseph E. and Sons, Inc. p. 92
Seaton, Mrs. Gordon p. 117
See, Holy p. 107
Seignorial, Chapter I, #4 (footnote) p. 159
Self, Mrs. John p. 119
Seminaries
   Diocesan Seminary of Nevan p. 105
   Holy Trinity Seminary p. 95
   Holy Trinity Seminary of Dallas p. 115
   Maynoth Seminary p. 73
   Mt. St. Mary's Seminary, Cincinnati, Ohio p. 72
   Our Lady of the Angels Seminary, Quincy, Illinois p. 97
   Seminary of the Barren's p. 107
   St. John's Diocesan Seminary of Little Rock p. 59
   St. John's Home Missions Seminary p. 78, 80, 82, 108
   St. John's Seminary p. 62, 74, 76, 95, 96, 98, 110, 147
   St. Mary's Seminary p. 112
   St. Patrick's Seminary, Menlo Park, Cal. p. 78
Sennet, Beulah p. 70
Sennett, Mrs. Beaulah p. 53
Series, Babe Ruth World p. 146
Services, Catholic Social p. 85, 87
Sesquicentennial in the State of Arkansas p. 7, 11
Settlement, St. Mary's p. 16
Settlements, Catholic p. 20
Seymore, Asa F. p. 53
Seymore, Mrs. Belle p. 53
Shannahan, Reverend Phillip p. 43, 71
Shares, Mrs. Agnes p. 53
Sheehy, Father p. 138
Sheehy, Reverend Patrick J. p. 138
Sherman, Joe p. 53
Sherry, Charles p. 53
Sherry, George p. 53
Sherry, Mrs. Mary p. 53
Shim, Prudentiana p. 133
Shinall, Mrs. Charles p. 133
Shinall, Mrs. C.P. p. 53
Shinall, Infant p. 133
Simmons, W.M. p. 53
Simpson, Alcinda p. 20
Simpson, Cornelia p. 20
Simpson, Frances p. 20
Simpson, J. p. 20
Simpson, Lucinda p. 20
Simpson, Maggie p. 133
Simpson, Thompson p. 20
Simpson, William p. 133

Sisters—Religious
   Mother Agnes Hart p. 19, 26
   Sister Adelaide Pendleton, S.C.N. p. 103
   Sister Angela, S.C.N. p. 133
   Sister Catherine Markey, M.H.S. p. 11
   Sister Charles Teresa, S.C.N. p. 102 (illus.), 103
   Sister Clarissa p. 133
   Sister Donald Mary Lynch, R.S.M. p. 92, 103, 104 (illus.)
   Sister Eudosia p. 133
   Sister Florence Yutterman, O.S.B. p. 145
   Sister Jane Frances Bey, D.C. p. 84 (illus.), 86 (illus.)
   Sister Maria Kleinschmidt, D.C. p. 88, 89 (illus.), 145
   Sister Mary Casimer, S.C.N. p. 103
   Sister Mary Catherine Dunn, D.C. p. 86, 87 (illus.)
   Sister Mary Leo, S.C.N. p. 67
   Sister Mary Sebastian p. 133
   Sister Mary Sylvan Tarver, S.C.N. p. 103
   Sister Patricia Bachman, D.C. p. 85 (illus.)
   Sister Placida p. 133
   Sister Silvia O'Brien, S.C.N. p. 116
   Sister Stephanie Hudek, D.C. p. 87, 88 (illus.)
   Sister Wallis p. 27
   Benedictine Sisters p. 107
   Sisters of Charity of Nazareth p. 62, 103, 104, 116, 117, 138
   Sisters of the Good Shepherd p. 108
   Sisters of Loretto p. 19, 29
   Sisters of Mercy p. 107
   Religious Sisters of Mercy p. 103, 110
   The Daughters of Charity of St. Vincent de Paul p. 84
Smidt, Charles p. 133
Smith, Arthur p. 53
Smith, Benjamin Franklin p. 35
Smith, B.F. p. 28
Smith, Clarence p. 53
Smith, Dr. C.D. p. 53
Smith, Mrs. C.D. p. 133
Smith, Mrs. Gertrude p. 53
Smith, Silas Joseph p. 133
Smith, Julius p. 53
Smith, Mrs. Louis p. 151
Smith, Miss Mary p. 53
Smith, Mrs. p. 53
Smith, Mrs. Mary p. 53
Smith, Joseph William p. 133
Smyrna p. 110
Society, Altar p. 67, 69, 151
Society, Altar, Officers 1945–46 p. 152 (illus.)
Society, Altar, Officers 1983–84 p. 152 (illus.)

191

Society, Ark. for Crippled Children p. 137
Society, St. Joseph's Altar p. 136, 150, 153
Soire, Baptiste p. 39
Soloman, Abraham p. 53
Soloman, Elias p. 53
Soloman, A. John p. 53
Southard, Miss Jessie Dean p. 153
South Carolina, Charleston p. 105
Spain p. 14, 35
Spaniards, the p. 13
Spousta, Charles p. 143
Spousta, Mary p. 143
Springs, Lee p. 142
Springs, Sulphur p. 142
Square, Court p. 34
St. Joseph's
  St. Joseph's p. 22, 46
  St. Joseph, Altar for p. 57
  St. Joseph's, Families of p. 11
  St. Joseph's, Laymen of p. 136
  St. Joseph's, Parish Board of Education p. 63
  St. Joseph's, Priests of p. 11
  St. Joseph's, Wardens of p. 60
  Staff, St. Joseph's p. 156–7 (illus.)
Stafford, Mrs. O.L. p. 158 (illus.)
Stahl, Jacob p. 133
Stahl, Joseph p. 133
Stanowski, Father C. p. 65
State, Boy's p. 146
State, Vatican City p. 96
States, United p. 14, 34, 35, 73, 107, 120
Statistics, Bureau of Vital p. 122
Stauder, Father Thomas p. 66
Steele, Joseph Aloyisuis p. 133
Steele, family p. 68, 119
Steele, Frank A. p. 147
Steele, Mrs. Frank p. 148
Steele, J. Leo p. 148
Steele, John p. 53
Steele, Miss Mary p. 53
Steele, Mrs. Mary p. 53
Steele, W.C. p. 133
Stephans, Alexander p. 37
Stone, Altar p. 57
Stone, Indiana white orletic p. 57
Stovecan, Ernest p. 53
Strager, Mrs. H.C. p. 133
Streets
  Alabama Street p. 39
  Broadway Street p. 44
  Dardenne Street p. 39
  Georgia Street p. 41
  Pullen Street p. 34, 41, 121
Striver, Barbara p. 133
Strobel, E. p. 53
Strobel, Frank p. 53
Stroble, Infant p. 133

Stroble, Joseph p. 133
Stroble, Maggie p. 134
Studies, Liturgical p. 68
Studies, Scripture p. 68
Studio, Lites
St. Beatrice, Chapter 9, #5 (footnote) p. 163
St. Benedict, the Order of p. 107
St. Elizabeth's Home for Girls p. 85
St. Francis Mission House, Forrest City, Ark. p. 78
St. Francis, the Poor Brothers of p. 110
Stillwell, Harold p. 16
St. Joseph's Cemetery Endowment Care Fund p. 121
St. Louis p. 15, 17, 19
St. Louis, Diocese of p. 15
St. Marie p. 22
St. Mary's p. 19, 22, 29, 46
St. Mary, Church of, Plum Bayou p. 7
St. Mary's Landing p. 22
St. Mary's, Plum Bayou p. 60
St. Patrick's, Sulphur Springs, Ark. p. 60
St. Stephen, chapel of p. 14
St. Stephen, the church of p. 15
Style, Byzantine p. 57
Style, Roman Basilica p. 57
Sullivan, C.J. p. 134
Sullivan, Eugene p. 134
Sullivan, Mrs. Ida p. 53
Sullivan, Mrs. p. 27
Sullivan, Robert p. 53
Surgeons, American College of p. 110
Suva, Charles p. 143
Swift, John p. 134
Sylvester, Mrs. Anna p. 53
Sylvester, Mrs. Anne p. 69
Sylvester, Antonio p. 134
Sylvester, Ben p. 53, 55
Sylvester, Ben A. p. 68
Sylvester, Charles p. 53
Sylvester, Charles H. p. 68
Sylvester, Mrs. Charles p. 134
Sylvester, family p. 119
Sylvester, Philamena p. 118 (illus.)
Sylvester, Mrs. Philumena p. 53
Sysmanszek, Annie p. 134
System, Arkansas Prison p. 91

T

Tabernacle p. 57
Taggart, Miss Alymer p. 53
Taggart, Augusta Cecelia p. 134
Taggart, Fred p. 134
Taggart, Guy p. 53
Taggart, Mrs. Marian p. 53
Taggart, M.H. p. 54

Taggart, W.O. p. 53, 54
Taggart, Mrs. W.O. p. 151
Taggart, Zelma Maria p. 134
Tague, J. p. 53
Tague, Miss Mary p. 53
Tague, Mrs. Mary p. 134
Tague, Paul p. 53
Tamaszewski, Miss Blanche p. 53
Tamaszewski, Caesar p. 53
Tamaszewski, Mrs. Frances p. 53
Tamaszewski, John p. 53
Tarver, John W. p. 103
Tarver, Rose Moore p. 103
Tarver, Sister Mary Sylvan,, C.S.N. p. 103
Tayler, Miss Jettie p. 53
Taylor, Ann C. p. 30
Taylor, Creed p. 19, 29, 30, 36, 37, 38, 120, 121
Taylor, Elizabeth p. 19
Taylor, Eulalia p. 19, 30
Taylor, Eulalie Vaugine p. 36, 37
Taylor, Lucille p. 134
Taylor, Mary p. 30
Taylor, Mary Ann p. 30
Taylor, N.P. p. 30
Taylor, Samuel p. 19
Taylor, Samuel C. p. 30
Taylor, S.C. p. 30
Taylor, Z. p. 30
Teague, Frank J. p. 134
Teems, (?), Mrs. Mary p. 134
Tenas, Frances p. 19
Tenas, Georginia p. 19
Tenas, Hiacinthe p. 19
Tenas, R. p. 19
Tennessee p. 37
Tennessee, Hendersonville p. 108
Tennessee, Memphis p. 95, 103
Tennessee, Nashville p. 108
Tennessee, Nashville, Vicar General of p. 108
Tennessee, Sumner County p. 108
Teresa, Sister Charles, S.C.N. p. 103
Territories
   Arkansas Territory p. 15
   Indian Territory p. 15, 21, 105
   Louisiana Territory p. 14, 15
   Northwest Territory p. 14
Terry, Charlie p. 53
Terry, Henry Clay p. 134
Terry, Francis p. 53
Terry, Mrs. H.C. p. 53
Terry, Infant p. 134
Texas p. 86
Texas, Dallas p. 92
Texas, San Antonio p. 72, 85
Texas, Weimer p. 87
Theilin, Mamie p. 134
Thessing, Mr. and Mrs. Theo., Sr. p. 68
Theolgian, of Bishop England p. 105
Theology p. 68
Theology, St. Meinrod School of p. 96
Thompson, Mrs. Agnes p. 53
Thompson, Clarence p. 134
Thompson, James p. 134
Thompson, Father John F. p. 65
Thompson, Father John J. p. 65
Thornhill, Mrs. C.E. p. 134
Tierney, Francis p. 134
Tierney, Joseph James p. 134
Tierney, John p. 134
Tierney, Mrs. John p. 134
Tierney, Patrick p. 53
Tierney, Peter M. p. 134
Tillman, Anna Roost p. 118 (illus.)
Timon, Reverend Mr. John p. 16
Timmons, William p. 134
Tomaszewski, John N. p. 134
Tomolunas, Father A. p. 65
Torres, Father p. 99
Torres, Mr. p. 98
Torres, The Reverend Robert A. p. 98, 101 (illus.)
Torres, Mrs. Trinidad p. 98
Travelers, United Commercial p. 137
Treasurer, Territorial p. 38
Treaty, Quapaw p. 20, 31, 33
Treutel, Infant p. 134
Tribes, Indian p. 35
Tribunal, Officialis of the Diocesan p. 80
Truehart, Edward p. 134
Truehart, J.E. p. 134
Tschann, Miss Liddie p. 53
Tuomy, Joseph p. 134
Turchi, Mrs. A. p. 153
Turchi, Aldo, family p. 70
Turchi, Chuck p. 147 (illus.)
Turchi, Mrs. Frances p. 153
Turchi, Mrs. Frank, Jr. p. 149
Turchi, Mrs. Joe p. 150
Turchi, Mrs. John p. 148
Turchi, Michael p. 147 (illus.), 148
Turchi, Mrs. Michael p. 148, 149 (illus.)
Turchi, Mrs. Theresa p. 153
Turkey p. 110
Turney, Infant p. 134
Tynin, Father p. 59, 60
Tynin, the Monsignor W.J., burse p. 147
Tynin, The Reverend Walter p. 57, 68
Tynin, Thomas A. p. 74
Tynin, The Very Reverend Monsignor Walter J. p. 74, 75

U

Ulte, Martin p. 134
Union, the p. 37
Unit, Women's Prison p. 88
United States p. 14, 34, 35, 73, 107, 120
United States, Apostolic Delegate to the p. 115
United States, the First Congress of p. 121
United States Soil Conservation Service p. 92
Unnamed p. 27
Unnamed, Infant p. 134
Utah p. 88

V

Vallier, Frances p. 19
Vallier, Francis p. 19
Vallier, F.D. p. 27
Vallier, Mary p. 19
Valliere, Augustine p. 36
Valliere, Bernard p. 35
Valliere, Elizabeth Augustine p. 36
Valliere, Eugenia p. 35
Valliere, Francois p. 35
Valliere, Don Joseph p. 35
Valliere, Joseph p.31, 35, 37
Valliere, Marie Ann p. 37
Valliere, Marie Augustine p. 36
Valliere, Marie Felicite p. 35, 36
Value, Joseph W. p. 27
Value, Mary p. 27
Vandeventer, Jacob p. 134
Vasseur, Etienne p. 15
Vatican p. 110
Vaughan, Grant p. 134
Vaughan, Samuel p. 134
Vaughn, Mrs. A.P. p. 53
Vaughn, Miss Frances p. 53
Vaugine p. 39
Vaugine, Audile p. 27
Vaugine, Audile Desruisseaux p. 36
Vaugine, Agnes B. p. 27
Vaugine, Benjamin p. 19
Vaugine, Caroline p. 134
Vaugine, Catherine O. p. 27
Vaugine, Celise p. 19
Vaugine, Celestine p. 19
Vaugine, Charles I. p. 27
Vaugine, Elizabeth p. 27
Vaugine, Etienette p. 36, 39
Vaugine, Etienne p. 36
Vaugine, Eulalie p. 36, 37
Vaugine, family p. 35, 37
Vaugine, Francis N. p. 27
Vaugine, F.N. p. 19, 27
Vaugine, Francois p. 36, 37

Vaugine, Frank G. p. 27
Vaugine, Grandfather p. 27
Vaugine, Grandmother p. 27
Vaugine, Harriet Wolfe p. 36
Vaugine, "His Little Daughter" p. 19
Vaugine, James p. 19
Vaugine, Louisine p. 19
Vaugine, Manette p. 36, 37, 38
Vaugine, Marie Felicite Valliere p. 36
Vaugine, Mrs. Mary p. 27
Vaugine, Mary E. p. 27
Vaugine, Mrs. Mary p. 37
Vaugine, Mathilde Desruisseaux p. 36
Vaugine, Monet p. 27
Vaugine, Mr. p. 18
Vaugine, Paul p. 19, 27, 36
Vaugine, Phillip N. p. 27
Vaugine, Stephen p. 27
Vaugine, M.T.R. p. 27
Vechia, Mary p. 134
Verret, E. p. 53
Verret, Edwin p. 134
Verret, Infant p. 135
Verret, J.T. p. 135
Verret, Mrs. Leana p. 53
Verret, Lucille p. 135
Verret, Orvil p. 135
Vicar General p. 108
Vicar General of Bishop England p. 105
Vincennes p. 14
Virgin, Blessed, Altar for p. 57
Virginia, Richmond p. 105
Vocations, Director of p. 61, 78
Vowell, Frank p. 135
Vowell, Mrs. Lena p. 53

W

Wadell, C.P. p. 53
Walker, Miss Beulah p. 53
Walker, Miss Eulalie p. 53, 135
Walker, James N. p. 135
Walker, J.M.C. p. 135
Walker, John M. p. 135
Walker, Joseph W. p. 135
Walker, Mrs. Nora p. 135
Walker, Robert Woods p. 135
Walker, Miss Virginia p. 53, 54
Wallis, Sister p. 27
Wallis, The Honorable Mr. Dave p. 11
Walshe, Alice p. 78
Walshe, Martin p. 78
Walshe, Monsignor p. 61, 78, 120, 121, 146
Walshe, Reverend Thomas F. p. 61
Walshe, The Very Reverend Thomas Francis p. 77
Walshe, The Very Reverend Monsignor Thomas Francis p. 77 (illus.)

Walter, John p. 135
Walters, Dottie p. 94
Walters, Father James p. 66
Ward, Mrs. Harold p. 117, 149
Wardens, Board of p. 60, 137
Wars
  Brooks—Baxter War p. 29
  Civil War p. 71, 107, 137
  World War II p. 61, 80, 137, 143
Washington, C. p. 20
Washington, Emily p. 20
Washington, Mary p. 20
Waskoski, Agnes p. 135
Waskoski, Mrs. Catherine p. 53
Waskoski, Ermine p. 135
Waskoski, Frederick p. 53
Waskoski, Henry p. 135
Waskoski, Infant p. 135
Waskoski, Joseph p. 53
Waskoski, Mrs. J. p. 53
Waskoski, Jun p. 53
Waskoski, Peter p. 135
Watson, George p. 20
Watson, Matilda p. 20
Watts, John R. p. 135
Watts, Oleale, family p. 119
Weaver, Mrs. Anna p. 53
Weaver, Mrs. Catherine p. 53
Weaver, Ernest p. 53
Weaver, Frank p. 135
Weaver, Katherine p. 135
Weaver, Lena p. 135
Weaver, Millard p. 53
Weaver, Millard J. p. 53
Weaver, Ralph Joseph p. 135
Weaver, Miss Thel p. 53
Weaver, Thomas G. p. 135
Webkes, Golden p. 67
Webkes, Mrs. Golden p. 53
Webkes, Henry p. 53, 67
Webkes, H.S., family p. 69, 70
Webkes, Infant p. 135
Webkes, Mr. John p. 11, 23, 24, 25, 41, 45, 60, 118
Wehr, Helen p. 110
Welch, R. p. 53
Wellman, Father William K. p. 66
Welsh, Patrick p. 135
Werling, Miss Anna p. 53
Werling, Mrs. Elizabeth p. 53
Werling, Francis p. 53
Werling, Frank p. 53
Werling, Mrs. Nellie p. 53
Werling, Oscar p. 53
Werling, Roy p. 53
Werling, Willie p. 135
Werner, Charles p. 135
West, Infant p. 135

West, Mount St. Mary's of the p. 107
Whelan, Bishop p. 105
White, Allan p. 53
White, Allen p. 22
White, Mrs. Emma p. 53
White, Mrs. Emma F. Vaugine p. 22
White, Mrs. J.B. p. 54
White, Mrs. Joe p. 151
White, Thomas p. 135
Whitley, Mollie Marshall p. 27
Whitworth, Mrs. Plunetta p. 135
Wilbert, Bill p. 148
Wilcox Amusement Co. p. 93
"Wilderness, Fletcher's" p. 112
Wilkins, Mrs. Mollie p. 53
Willerman, Mrs. Louise p. 135
Williams, B. p. 53
Williams, Mrs. B. p. 53
Williams, C.F. p. 135
Williams, Mrs. Etta p. 53
Williams, John B. p. 135
Williams, Joe p. 53
Williams, Joseph p. 135
Williams, Ramon p. 53
Williams, Warren p. 53
Williamson, Mr. C. Frank p. 11
Windham, T.C. p. 139
Window, composite p. 48 (illus.)
Window, Pastor's Memorial p. 46 (illus.)
Window, Saracen p. 48 (illus.), 49
Window, Saracen's original p. 47 (illus.)
Winfrid, —— p. 53
Winkler, Jeff p. 147 (illus.)
Winter, Mrs. Mary p. 135
Wise, Mrs. G.W. p. 135
Wise, Infant p. 135
Wise, Mrs. Mary p. 53
Withers, Miss Josephine p. 53
Withers, Mrs. Julia p. 53
Wolf, Mrs. Ethel p. 135
Wolfe, Harriet p. 36
Wolff, Mrs. R.C. p. 53
Wood, Chris p. 150
Wood, Eleanorae p. 142
Wood, Elizabeth p. 142
Wood, Emma p. 142
Wood, Mrs. Guy p. 135
Wood, Infant p. 142
Wood, Mary p. 142
Wood, Sarah E. p. 142
Wood, W.H. p. 142
Woods, J. p. 53
Woolford, Infant p. 135
Works, Pine Bluff Iron p. 136
Wright, Mrs. A.M. p. 53
Wright, Charles p. 53
Wright, Mrs. J.B. p. 135
Wright, Pauline p. 135

Wright, Mrs. Stella p. 53
Wright, Miss Winfrid p. 53

Y

Young, Miss p. 20
Young, Mr. p. 20
Young, Mrs. David p. 155 (illus.)
Yutterman, Sister Florence, O.S.B. p. 145

Z

Zemek, Paul p. 142